The Energy
of Life

A Guide To Healing and Balancing from Within

Jennifer Kaye

3rd Generation Intuitive

Copyright © 2011 Jennifer Kaye
All Rights Reserved

No part of this book may be reproduced in any form or by any electronic or mechanical means including information storage and retrieval systems, without permission in writing from the author.

ISBN: 978-1-4276-5326-0

CONTENT

PREFACE vii

INTRODUCTION xi

Chapter 1. THE STABILITY ENERGY CENTER 1

Chapter 2. THE PASSION ENERGY CENTER 17

Chapter 3. THE SELF ASSURANCE ENERGY CENTER 37

Chapter 4. THE LOVE ENERGY CENTER 61

Chapter 5. THE COMMUNICATION ENERGY CENTER 89

Chapter 6. THE INTUITIVE ENERGY CENTER 105

Chapter 7. THE WISDOM ENERGY CENTER 123

Chapter 8. ENERGIES THAT DESTROY HOPE, HEALTH, AND WELL-BEING 145

Illusional Energy *145*

Expectation Energy *157*

Story Energy *171*

EPILOGUE 187

ACKNOWLEDGMENTS 211

ABOUT THE AUTHOR 215

The team *216*

Jennifer Kaye empowerment Collection *221*

"It is not what is done to us in this lifetime that matters the most.

It is what we do to ourself that is everlasting."

Jennifer Kaye
1989

PREFACE

My name is Jennifer Kaye and I specialize in reading energy associated with imbalances within the physical, mental, emotional, and spiritual components of the human body and psyche. With the natural gift of intuition, I am able to accurately detect challenges that can make us feel/become ill, anxious, out-of-sorts, or disconnected with the energy of our personal power and life force. For over 13 years, I have worked closely with numerous private clients and licensed health care professionals to create an infrastructure of vital information that assists both individuals, practitioner, and patient in understanding the underlying reasons for dysfunction, illness, stagnation, and unbalanced thoughts and feelings.

My unique gift also attracts those who have a desire to achieve greater abundance, personal understanding, closer emotional relationships, and success in achieving short and long-term goals. The ability to share an accurate insight into the internal challenges that are not always obvious and are often misunderstood and misdiagnosed can have a huge impact on those seeking to move forward toward optimum health, harmony within, and sense of consistent well-being.

It's been an incredible journey for me personally while I've explored my intuitive gift. Moving forward, though a bit confusing at times, I found my place in an area that I have found fascinating and rewarding. I have pursued my work with great enthusiasm, awe, and wonder. My passion revolves around working with the 7 major energy centers. Over the years, my grasp of these centers has grown in clarity and depth. Being able to *actually* see and feel the energy stored in these very powerful energy centers from human birth continues to intrigue me even today, after all these years.

I share this profoundly effective and insightfully charged roadmap of health and harmony with you today with the desire to empower you. I want you to explore these energy centers on your own. By following the signs and signals of your own energy, you will find the personal connection to a life that can be filled with excitement, hope, love, passion, and fulfillment. With the support of so many who have experienced real personal healing and understanding through my gift and understanding, and the sincere connection I have to humanity, I have created this book to provide practical and profound guidance for those who seek a better understanding of how they can participate with and empower their own inner wisdom, and those on the road toward balance and personal well-being. To live in this life with a greater understanding of *how* you affect your own life is priceless.

I believe we all hold the answers to personal happiness and an overall feeling of joy and contentment within ourselves. This feeling holds a different interpretation for all of us. Discovering your interpretation of what you want in your life, and pursuing it, is one of the most sought-after concepts of this century. To truly find your bliss, your comfort, and your connection to personal happiness is one of the most important findings you will encounter in your lifetime. The roadmap of the 7 major energy centers that we all embody can assist us to understand this. If we choose to listen and learn how to read the clues and apply them to our daily lives, we can connect to our personal power, our truth, and the wisdom we have inside. Our incredible bodies have so much to teach us when we just learn to listen. The illustration on the next page shows you where these major energy centers reside in our body. In addition, there are 4 other minor energy centers locating in the centers of our palms and soles which are quite highly active energetically as well.

My gift of intuition allows me to help those who have tried various methods of understanding imbalances in their lives. Accessing information has always been the easy part of my work. Feeling the pain, frustration, anger, and total helplessness of those sitting in front of me, year after year, created an opportunity for me to expand my ability to be of service to a larger audience.

As you read through the pages, please take a long pause to familiarize yourself with the energy center locations within your own body. It is my hope that you discover within yourself a deeper understanding of how energy is stored and expressed in your own seven main energy centers. These centers affect each of us on a very conscious and unconscious level.

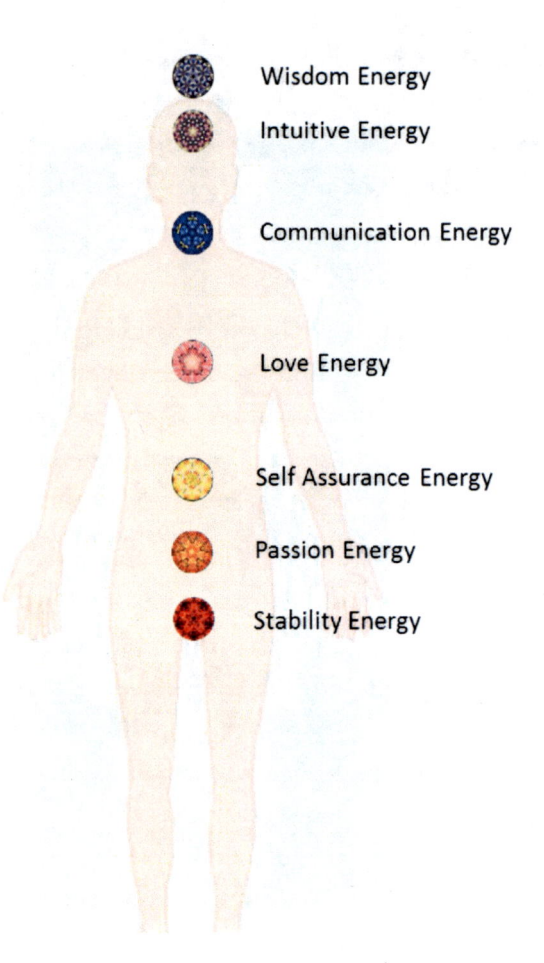

- Wisdom Energy
- Intuitive Energy
- Communication Energy
- Love Energy
- Self Assurance Energy
- Passion Energy
- Stability Energy

THE 7 ENERGY CENTERS

Connecting You to Your Inner Truth

Jennifer Kaye Energy System Chart
Empowerment Series™

INTRODUCTION

Energy Affects Us in Profound and Personal Ways, Knowingly or Unknowingly

Many of us continue to repeat the same patterns, never quite accessing the feelings we desire, the goals we set, or the diligence necessary to maintain consistent well-being or to find true success. For many, thoughts, expectations, and intense energy can create self-sabotage. Without needing to analyze the reasons why, these patterns and *hit-and-miss* moments can pile up leading to disappointment, frustration, anger, illness, or the inability to have positive momentum.

Energy, and how we use it, see it, feel it, and apply it, can hold the key to many unanswered questions. To understand the effects of energy, you must first understand its essence. How we interact, react, respond, and engage all involves the essence of energy.

Human energy, the essence of who we are as a living being, is the thought (mental energy) and emotion/feeling that flows within ourself and interacts with others in each moment.

Our mind (mental thoughts) and feelings (our emotions) direct us from the second we awake. Think about that. Please sit with that for a moment. When you wake up, how do you plan your day? What is the first step? It is thought, feelings, repetition, memory, and action. And we are on our way. Our thoughts have an energetic effect upon the people in our lives as well as an effect on ourself. We use energy positively or negatively on a daily basis. It is that simple. We use it positively to benefit ourself and those around us, or we can, unfortunately, use it negatively, often times without knowing it.

Energy is working for you or against you. Thoughts you feel today can have lasting effects that you are not always aware of. If you have repeated thoughts, as most of us do, you may already be aware of how they can work with or against you. Normally, we either feel healthy, successful, and balanced or we feel tired, overwhelmed, and stressed. For most of us, maintaining stability in our positive thoughts and feelings can sometimes be overshadowed by the enormous stress carried throughout our lives. I have found that direct thoughts aren't always the culprit of our dis-ease. Many times, it's an unconscious thought attached to many old feelings and memories of experiences that creates the distress. Even though I've heard, time and time again, the phrase: "No, Jennifer, I've worked through that," whether they are sitting in front of me or on the telephone talking to me, most of what they *thought* they had worked through is still very much alive, under the layers of *positive* thinking! It can be very confusing. Why am I not healing? Why don't I feel better? What is wrong with me? These are viable real questions that deserve a complete and thorough answer and understanding. Imagine a storage box filled with all of the events that have occurred in our lives, like a memory bank of sorts. That is the image I see and access through my gift of intuition. This is the reason the 7 energy centers have such an impact on me personally. The energy centers hold memories from birth. I am able to access the memory box of individuals who look for deeper understanding to life's challenges. I'm quite sure many of us do not understand how this could be possible. Well, I can honestly say, I was a bit confused myself. Let me give you examples so you may understand what I am referring to. Do you know what triggers thoughts that you have not felt for ages? Do you understand what happens internally, without thought or direction, when you hear an old song that brings up memories? How can you possibly remember or, more importantly, *feel* on any given day, any given moment, a sensation from, and sometimes full memory of, exactly where you were, who you were with, what you felt, and how you still feel it all today when you hear a song? It has been stored. An example of what you wanted to feel and remember is understandable, but what about the feelings, memories, and moments that are less desirable to remember? We access knowingly with purpose when we want them those that will serve us positively. We unknowingly react and respond, without thought, when we least expect, to those less desirable, those we want to forget.

This is similar to the unseen energy that I am describing. Information is stored within the energy centers of us. Often times, many of us are searching for answers to satisfy our goals that never seem to be reached. We try to attract positive relationships but often find little success, or we involve in work that does not provide a sense of fulfillment, without the belief that we can make changes that would actually be successful and beneficial to us on so many levels of our lives. These imbalances can, and are, caused by our internal thought processes.

You may ask, "Why is it important to understand the connection between the energy of the mind and the body?" Why is there a need to understand the energy associated with thoughts and feelings? My opinion is that our thoughts and feelings *are* energy. This energy affects how we see life, how we interact with ourselves and others, and most importantly, even sadly for those who cannot find peace, how we move through our very precious life. This energy also affects how much pleasure and joy we can feel and how well we understand our true self.

Operating at optimal capacity, the human spirit resides in this physical body with strength, clarity, joy, feeling of love, and a sense of purpose. Operating from a place without hope, passion, desires, or love, the human spirit can, and will, diminish its powerful life force. How we interact in our lives affects us. How we see life affects us. This is *'The Energy of Life'* I will be referring to throughout the book.

Do you achieve the desired results in your work? Do you receive the confirmation, love, and compassion from those you love and support? Do you live without expectation thus receiving gifts unconditionally from those who surround you? Or, have you learned to have expectations that are rarely met? Expectations that we feel are never met or will ever be met can set us up for constant and consistent depression and anxiety. We are waiting for the moment that we believe, consciously or unconsciously, will never appear. What if you were to learn that our thought and the energy behind the thought can, and will, remove all possibility of obtaining those desires?

Our thoughts interact with us each moment. The energy within us is felt throughout our environment and our everyday life. Our energy, the essence of us, has an immediate and direct effect on those around us. Our family, our mate or spouse, our children, our co-workers, and even the people who serve us in our favorite restaurant can be affected by our energy. We are the energy we give to others. Take a pause for just a minute: *We Are the Energy We Give To Others.* What does that look like and feel like for you? Right now, at this moment in your life. What would happen if you took charge of the energy you extend? And somehow direct it to benefit yourself and those who you care for?

Have you ever been around someone who is always happy and always positive? How about spending time with someone who is always complaining, always talking about the same issues and the same problems? The energy associated with us can bring happiness and success or discomfort and stress. It is associated with the ability to obtain and reach our goals, or the feeling of being let down, or always being exhausted or consistently frustrated. How can that be possible?

Listen to Your Inner True Self

Take a moment to breathe into that answer. If you have religion in your belief system, you will recognize it as the spirit of oneself. If you have theory thinking within, you may see it as character or personality. It all comes down to the essence of ourself; *the energy of you!* Each of our family members has an energy, personality, or spirit. Each of our friends, lovers, partners, spouses, etc. has an energy field. We either enjoy and feel supported or feel frustrated, unworthy, and disconnected by the energy of those we surround ourselves with.

When we take the original or initial essence of ourself and add the experiences and moments of our life, we can then see how we arrived at *us*. This combination of our true essence and our life experiences allows us to arrive at who we truly are! We as individuals are like no other. Embrace that about yourself. Embrace the powerful energy of being a unique you! When we understand our true self, can we embrace the power within.

How do we interact in our world? Only we know deep inside if we are presenting our true self to the world and those around us or if we hide our feelings and thoughts to adjust to what the world and those in it would like us to be. The energy of our true self does not have confusion. Accessing our true self allows us to know, utilize, and grow the internal power and resources we have available. This power, this incredible energy source, is available to each and every one of us. When we sift or weed out what is not necessary, we can become our true self. For some, the task of knowing oneself and expressing oneself honestly and openly can be rather difficult, especially if a *persona* has been set up. Or for those who lack self-confidence, or feel they are trapped in their world.

Understanding the power of your essence, the energy of you, can become a barometer or a measuring stick that allows us to gauge and positively manipulate our energy and the energy we use with others. Using this powerful personal tool can be as simple as applying your make-up or combing your hair. Just as we learned to operate our vehicle, interact with friends, or create a bond with our lover or spouse, we can create a personal relationship and awareness with the energy of ourself.

The Roadmap to Balance and Harmony

There is a very unique system or roadmap, as I like to call it, associated with the entire human body/mind/spirit. The system is often named the "chakra system," made up of the 7 main energy centers that I have been referring to. For thousands of years, it has been used as a vehicle to diagnose imbalances within the mental, physical, emotional, and spiritual components of one's self. Although the first documented understanding of the energy system was identified in India during 2000-600 B.C., modern physiology allows us to actually observe that these 7 energy centers correspond exactly to the seven main nerve ganglia which emanate from the spinal column. By learning to read the energetics of each center, one can access valuable wisdom that allows the individual to tap into resources available to address physical challenges and emotional or mental disorders. This tapping in can promote a high level of connection toward maintaining harmonious balance and joyful living. The creator, of this incredible planet and all that embraces life here on earth, did not leave us to fend for ourselves without having an internal strength and insightful knowing for healing ourselves. This body we live in has incredible healing abilities. Our spirit is connected to the physical body. Hearing our spirit, understanding the energy of ourself, and applying that wisdom to our everyday life is an incredible platform to enjoy.

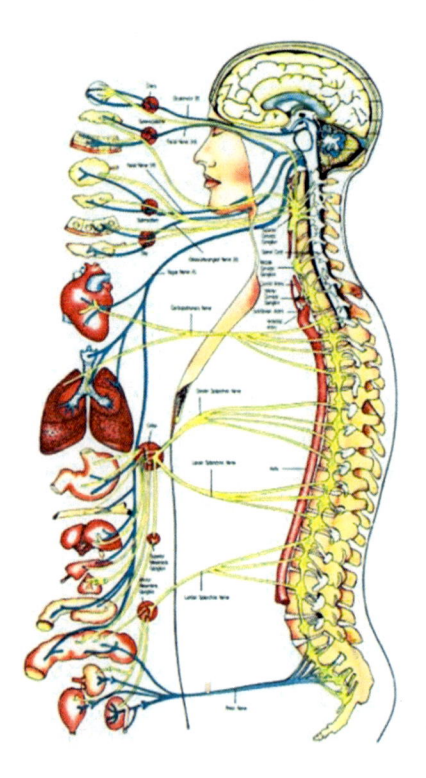

The central nervous system (CNS) which consists of the brain and the spinal cord connects to, receives the information from, and interacts with all parts of the body through billions of neurons. The imbalance or dysfunction of our physical body leads to physical discomfort which leads to emotional and mental distress. On the other hand, the imbalance or dysfunction of the energy centers, which surfaces through our feelings, could also result in physical dis-ease, mediating, initially mainly, through the endocrine system.

Over the years, I have developed a profound understanding of the energy associated with these centers and believe that they are valuable resources for getting to know and understand our entire beings. Even a rudimentary understanding of these energy centers can provide simple answers to often complex challenges. This book will give you the basics so that you can identify your own 7 main energy centers and tune into what they are telling you by how they express themselves physically (with symptoms) and emotionally (with feelings). I will guide you with story and simple techniques to help you access what I've learned to enhance every part of your life, both internally and externally.

Today, numerous hospitals, clinics, and high profile physicians are beginning to finally integrate these subtle energy modalities into their practice and facilities. John Hopkins Medical Center, The Mayo Clinic, Columbia University Medical Center, Harvard Medical School, and many other world renowned providers are finding patient satisfaction and successful outcome based upon Eastern medicine and the various "energy medicine" techniques.

Imagine that during one of the worst recession periods reported in the entire history of America, the public spent over 33.9 billion dollars on "unconventional" treatment along with 5.3 billion on supplements and herbal remedies. Hundreds of thousands of people are finding tremendous relief and benefits from these resources and valuable tools. Understanding the effects of energy on our total living system and applying wisdom and practical application are wonderful and effective ways to reap the immediate benefits.

Living in harmony requires nothing more than truly listening to ourself.

Understanding the 7 energy centers allows access to balancing the mind, body, and spirit!

What Is Really Going On Inside?

Energy can often affect us without our knowing or agreeing to it. Think about a time when you answered your phone, feeling optimistic and upbeat. Then, somehow, within a minute or less of hearing the voice, just the voice, of a person you were in conflict with, estranged from, or emotionally or mentally entangled with, your entire mental, emotional or physical self shifted. Now, remember a time you began a conversation with someone and within seconds you found yourself crossing your hands over your stomach or upper chest in a kind of act of protection. Without our consent or approval, we participate with the energy in our lives. That means we not only soak in the easy, healthy energy but the toxic and debilitating as well. Many people find relief when they start to understand that they can take the reins and feed themselves the energetic nutrition they crave just by paying attention to what is going on in their 7 energy centers.

Consider a few more common examples of how energy can invade you without your awareness. Have you ever had to prepare yourself to meet with someone you are afraid of or feel angry at? Have you found yourself with a headache or a pain in your neck and had to self-medicate? Do you ever find yourself needing to breathe deeply to relax before a meeting with a boss, someone who consistently creates a feeling of *uneasiness* within you? We can argue that it is *them* causing our dis-ease or pain.

But in essence, it is *us*. It is us responding to their energy from our own energy imbalance. When we are in balance energetically and when we have our body in alignment with our mind and spirit, the energy that surrounds us does not affect us in the debilitating ways as it can, and will, when we are unbalanced.

The spirit of our human self lives within the incredible shell we call the human physical body. It is an extraordinary vehicle we are driving. Although we rarely acknowledge this incredible body until we become challenged or ill, it is here, available, and willing to assist us in understanding our true inner self. Yes, it is the key to discovering so many powerful answers about who we are. All we need to do to participate with this God given equipment is *listen!*

Our body provides signals to let us know when and what we need. If we keep our spirit and our body fluid and balanced, we can live in harmony with ourselves, and with little effort. If we start to challenge our spirit, our true self, by ignoring the signs and signals sent to us from our physical body, we will live in an imbalanced and often unhealthy state of affairs.

In today's very fast paced world, we, as a community here in the United States, are spending over 11 billion dollars on what is often called "Healing, Health, and Wellness." What does this tell us? We are starting to wake up as a society! We are trying to connect to our *feelings* of illness and unease. We want to know what's going on. We want to have access to what's real and important for our lives. We want to be more.

Acknowledge Your Surroundings - Feel the Environment

Have you ever walked very slowly and consciously through an aquarium, botanical garden, or bird sanctuary? Have you ever noticed the incredibly intricate and perfect skin, feathers, and features of these magnificent creatures that inhabit the planet? They occupy the same breathing and living space as we do. They seem to live in a kind of elegant harmony; they seem to be at ease and at one. It is difficult to sit with this profound awareness when we are all so consumed by life's demands and responsibilities. I suggest you take a moment to soak in the beauty and balance of nature: the animals, the plants, the flowers, scenery, all of it. Choose what you are attracted to. You will feel not only an energetic connection, but a sense of peace and comfort. This peace, this visible balance is available to all of us if we will take the time and extend the effort to pay attention and listen. Have you ever wondered why the most sought-after healing and wellness centers are in and surrounded by *nature* settings? Why clinics and healing professionals line their offices with plants, water fountains, nature sounds, and as close to natural surroundings as possible? It's the energy that feeds and heals our souls naturally! Be in nature as often as you can. Don't wait for the family or personal vacation. Find a place near you right now that you can sit in or walk through as often as possible. Don't fit it in once a year or when you have vacation time. Or, sadly, when you become so ill you must take the time off to heal.

I invite you to take this journey with me, while paying closer and more loving attention to this remarkable vehicle we call our bodies. To be gentle and loving to our soul, our spirit, regardless of what it is feeling, through acknowledgement. Soon, you will be able to apply what you learn to a deeper knowing of how to make your life flow with joy and ease. Even when you experience the moments of sadness, tragedy, unhappiness, despair, and discomfort (which is upon each and every one of us as human spirits), you will find your way back to balance more quickly, with greater ease and a deeper understanding. That is what we all strive for, isn't it? To be able to get back to a sense of balance when life's moments and experiences take us off guard. Life experience continues daily. We know it is really about choices, decisions, reaction, and action. Life experiences do not only affect us from our seat in life. The experiences of those we love and interact with also affect us on a very deep level. Learning how to process our experiences and the experiences that naturally affect us from those around us allow us to move forward with energy that can, and will, empower the balance within.

Why feel out of sorts with yourself or with others? Why sabotage yourself with the frustrations of being disorganized or unable to get from here to there? Why settle for being exhausted or overwhelmed? Why accept chronic illness? Why live a life without your dreams and goals coming true? When you tap into your 7 main energy centers and learn how to listen, read, and respond to them, you will find your life transformed and your inner wisdom growing. Looking for extra energy? Do you desire the special connection to optimal well-being? Or, do you want to live without chaos and constant frustration?

It's an exciting journey if you're up for the ride!

Misconception of Life Energy

One huge misconception of life and its ups and downs is the unrealistic idea that we should always be happy. How can we possibly be happy all the time? Life is ever changing. Our environments are ever changing. Our relationships are ever changing as well as the people in our lives. We as human spirits are here to experience life, experience the truth of ourselves. A better word for what we would like to achieve on a daily basis might be: *balance*. A feeling of balance or stability as often as possible is what we might strive to feel; a sense of balance as often as we can. Life happens and is happening all around us. It is happening to us, to those in our community, in our inner circle, and within our families. To those we love, to those we care for, to those who protect us and love us, to those who financially support us, and more.

Energy is affecting them at the same rate it is affecting us. We are not isolated in this movement of daily life energy. To wonder why we are not happy all of the time is unrealistic. It simply adds more pressure to us. It can, because of all we have heard from the media and print publications, create a feeling of depression and despair if we are not always *up* and happy. What happens when your husband or wife or child or friend wakes up and unexpectedly feels bad, depressed, angry, or just out of place? How does that affect your energy? How quickly do we want them to "snap out of it" so we can all be *happy*?

Creating a sense of balance is a goal most of us are able to accept and strive towards on a consistent basis. Learning how to *not react* in a way that causes unnecessary stress and illness to ourselves and those around us is doable for most. Striving for balance, without too much reaction, is better suited for most human beings. Especially with all we have endured in our lifetime. A little balance now and then would be great, right? Life is an experience we are all here to participate in. We go through many emotional experiences during our lifetime. We triumph from time to time in our lifetime. We have experiences we will never forget, good and bad, throughout our lifetime, as does every other human being on this planet. I've never heard nor known a human being who has had a *perfect* life. Have you?

Welcome to 'The Energy of Life' Guidebook - How to Use This Book

Over the years I have seen thousands of individuals one-on-one. My purpose has been to provide them with specific information to help them find answers to questions that are at times unseen, unresolved, or misunderstood. *The Energy of Life* is a guidebook that gives *you* the knowledge and tools necessary to help you apply much of my work to your own current situations and life challenges. If you've picked up this book, you are someone who is looking for answers by putting the ultimate responsibility in your own hands to make the changes and shifts that are important to you! Having the insight necessary to understand your inner self is priceless.

Throughout these pages, my goal is to teach you about the 7 main energy centers. I want you to get to know the incredible energy and insight you have available to yourselves; to know you have *easy* access to valuable information that can be instantly applied on a daily basis. With the wellness challenges we face today, it is imperative to have access to the inner wisdom and power we have available to us. Living in the world today can be overwhelming. Most of us are not living; we are trying to keep up, to survive. Unfortunately, as a society and in most communities, we are so overwhelmed that we feel we are in constant *battle* on a daily basis. It is an energy we have created mentally and are now responding emotionally and physically. Although it seems as though it may be just too simple, you must understand that the *blueprint* of this human experience and the human body are linked together. We are not here to struggle as much as we think or have been taught. Our body is the key to understanding our emotions, mental energies, and many physical challenges. Our creator did not drop us into this life in order to undertake these life lessons and experiences without a road map or a body to support our human experience. I intend to start you on your path or, for those seasoned veterans, to help you understand and remember just how simple and accessible things that you truly need are in order to build balance from within.

The intention of this book is to offer guidance, as you come to understand how energy affects you both positively and negatively. As you learn about each of the 7 main energy centers, as well as find out more about Illusion Energy, Expectation Energy, and Story Energy, you will discover more and more about yourself and how to embrace life's energies in beneficial and healthy ways.

Knowledge is one piece of the puzzle. Feeling is the other part, which I believe is almost more important than the intellectual side of the teaching. I invite you to bring *all* of yourself to this process: your mind, body, and spirit. And, I encourage you to trust that you will learn to reconnect to your inner source of wisdom, insight, and your own body's resources--the signs and signals that will alert you to what is truly brewing within your entire system.

Use this book any way that feels right to you. Read it from beginning to end or just pick it up and open it up randomly. I do encourage you to actively commit to participate in just one activity after one of the chapters, the chapter of your choice. Try it just for the experience. I hope you will find the book to be simple, elegant, and perhaps a profound resource that is transformational and will serve you well.

YOUR PERSONAL BODY CHART

To get started, I suggest you take a few moments to notate any pains, challenges, or discomfort in your own body. Use the following chart as a tool to document any challenges or weak spots. You may be quite surprised to find out what areas of your body are linked to the 7 major energy centers. Please refer to this chart as you read this book to help you begin to understand what imbalances you hold within your own body, mind, and spirit.

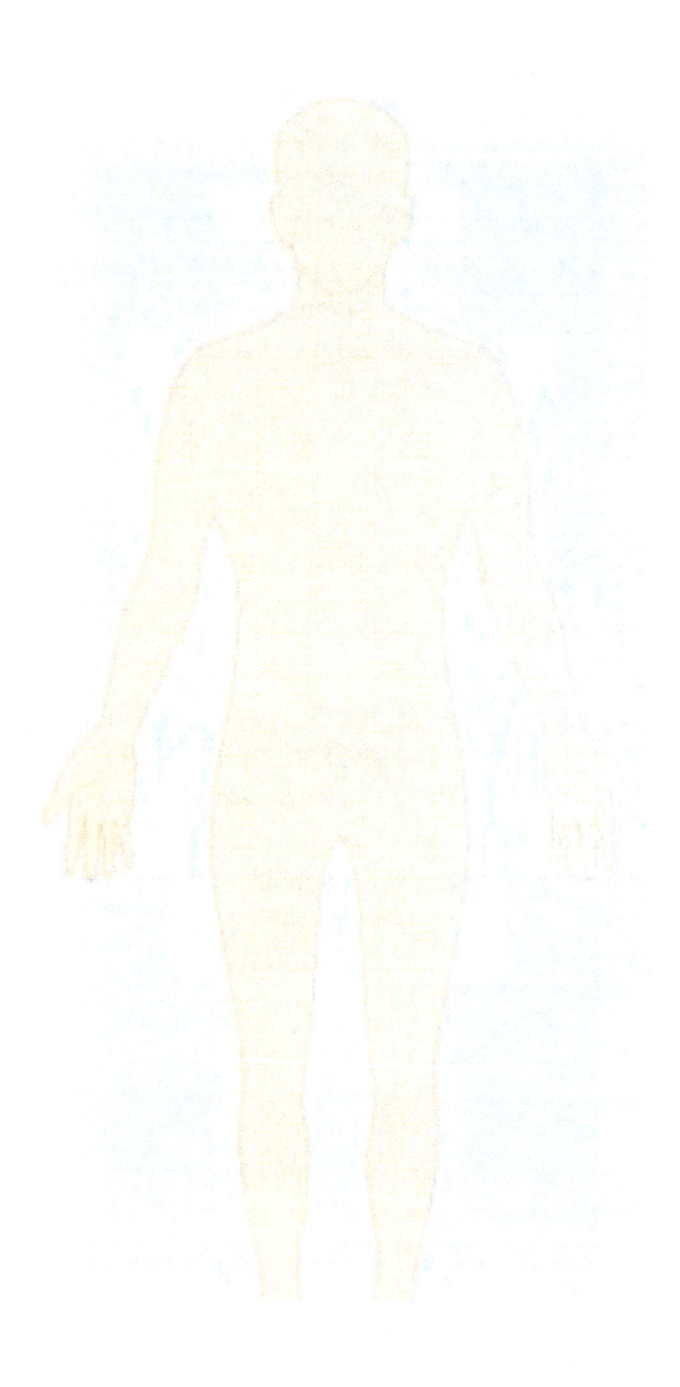

Chapter 1.

THE STABILITY ENERGY CENTER

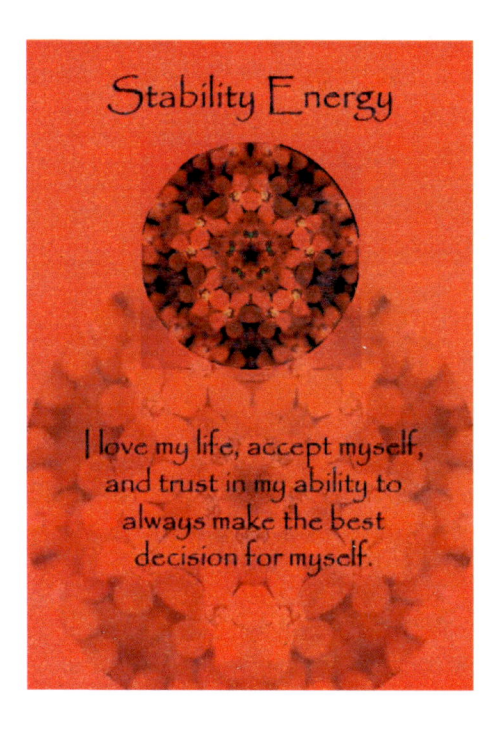

Stability Energy

I love my life, accept myself, and trust in my ability to always make the best decision for myself.

Significance: This energy center must be balanced for the other energy centers to align properly. Stability energy is our ability to create security within our core. Sound decision making. Feeling a sense of internal balance. Feeling rooted in the decisions you've made or will make. Feeling confidence to move forward with life, choices, past decisions, and results.

Balanced: We have met our basic security, survival, and stability issues. Feelings of satisfaction and comfort.

Unbalanced: We feel unstable, uprooted, indecisive, and restless. We can have panic feelings, a feeling of despair, and a feeling of helplessness. A feeling of being stuck and not having the answers to move forward. Inability to balance oneself in mental structures that supporting forward movement. A real or an illusion sense of feeling stuck without options. Inflammation of feet, knees, lower legs, or joints can be a challenge of the stability energy.

❦❧❦❧❦❧❦❧❦❧

The Stability or Root Energy Center is attached to feeling stable. It is also associated with our physical attraction to others and defines how we move through the world. Do we have a clear sense of survival and sexual stability? Do we manifest abundance on all levels, including financial success and emotional fulfillment? How open and in the flow we are is defined by how balanced we are in our Stability Energy Center. Being balanced in this center makes a big difference in how secure we actually feel walking the planet. If our energy is not moving in this center, we also may feel stuck, frozen, and unable to move.

The Root or Stability Energy Center is the foundation of the entire energy system network. The *energy* of this center extends downward, from the hips through the legs, knees, ankles, and feet. Trouble in these particular areas can be traced back to our *inability* to move forward or move with ease within one's life circumstances. Lower back problems are also associated with this energy center. When the blockage is severe, the person literally struggles with issues of movement, is wary to take risks, and loses self-confidence. The body responds with pain and, at times, severe discomfort. The Stability Energy Center is then locked and not alive or responding. It is often stuck in a pattern of deep fear. It is not surprising that this center oversees core survival issues as well; issues such as eating, sleeping, exercise, and securing the financing to take care of yourself or others. It defines the essential feeling of safety and security within your environment.

If there are challenges in this energy center, you can repeat the same patterns of instability over and over. You may find yourself changing jobs, relocating, suffering from chronic health issues, weight fluctuations, anxiety, fear of the future, and the inability to make choices to better your current circumstances. What I have described is a repeated pattern that indicates this energy center is out of balance. Again, when this particular energy center is out of balance, it is a direct reflection of your inability to feel safe and secure.

People who have challenges in this area have difficulty with intimacy in sex, meaning that their attraction to the sexual experience holds relatively no emotional component. It also shows up as the feeling of greed, never feeling satisfied, never having enough. Sadly, a person who has challenges with this energy center often searches endlessly for answers and rarely finds fulfillment, until they directly deal with the energy center and get it to "defrost" and mobilize again, so that they can move forward.

When you recognize that you must move forward, you actually have to shake yourself from your sense of being "frozen," out-of-sorts, or in a state of discontent so that you can admit and face your own instability. It isn't always easy. I've worked with many men and women struggling with this energy center who basically need real "prying" to get them to move out of being stuck.

The Energy of 'Nature'

Is it really that simple? Be in Nature? An incredibly strong energetic field of healing/balancing capabilities that can have an immediate effect on the human energy field is nature. It's that simple. How do you feel when you take a trip to the beach, a mountain, the desert, or a place filled with trees? Our body and mind crave nature! It is a very important piece of our connection to our inner self. It cannot be overlooked as a tool for balance and reorganization. It can take you to a place of *silence* and *calm*.

One way to get things moving and flowing again is to reconnect with nature. The earth, dirt, trees, grass, and plants all provide a link to grounding oneself. Walking outside on the sand or grass and staying away from pavement or cement can pull the energy that is encased in the lower part of the body downward. Many clients ask *why* the ground provides support. I believe it has to do with the magnetic connection to the inner core of the earth's base. If you look at the lifeline of many powerful trees such as cedar, fir, eucalyptus, birch, and oak, you will notice that they flourish regardless of the many catastrophes that surround them. The earth's core is a balance for all who reside on its surface. How do you feel when you head up to the mountains? Desert? Ocean? Our connection to the ground, the core that sustains us, can be a great benefit.

When we struggle with limitation in our Stability Energy Center, we need to see it as an impetus to connect with beauty, power, and the awe of nature. The natural world will counteract the time we've spent immersed in the darkness and limbo of the *survival* or *fear* mode and will literally ground us again. It will allow our energy to then rise up our bodies and circulate. It is a key to balancing our mind, body, and spirit.

Why does This Energy Center Become So Unbalanced?

How does our *stability* become so fragile, so disconnected, so removed from ourselves? Life challenges can really impact the Stability Energy Center. Here are a few key areas that can cause the energy to become distorted, confused, and unbalanced:

- Divorce or separation from a loved one.
- Introduction of a child or children with or without planning.
- Denial of child bearing for men and women with the desire to create a family.
- Denial of an emotional stress that does not have a satisfactory resolution.
- Children leaving the nest.

- Career loss.

- Abusive behavior by a spouse, child, or significant person in your environment, that has caused severe despair, loss of self, removal of sense of security and clarity of reality association.

- Feeling low self-worth.

- Multiple parenting as a child.

- Loss of a loved one.

- Aging without Purpose, Security, or Meaning.

- Stagnation with Work, Love, and Freedom of Expression.

- Addiction at an early age.

- Aging with the feeling that the *best* is behind and not yet-to-come.

- Unforeseen health issue affecting you or a family member.

- Death of a child or an important person close to you.

The truth is that these major changes in life, challenges in life, and the essence of the severe impact they have had can contribute to life-long struggles. To downplay episodes of how we deal with tragedy, change of life, abuse (regardless of the type), and other emotional and mental trauma is simply foolish.

To believe that in *a moment* it can feel better with some form of instant *self-help* dictation, without acknowledging the *core* challenge or experience, is hard for me to believe. I've watched, time and time again, the stuffing of the emotions attached to these painful experiences. The first step in healing or moving forward is to identify what will and will not work for you personally. Healing is a state of understanding and conscious movement. It is essential that you plan for it according to your individual background, current life situation, history of emotional contentment, and the core condition of your immune system. For this reason alone, herein lies the reason we must look at healing from an individual point of view.

There are many factors in healing and moving forward. We are all here to experience various lessons in life. We are in no hurry. Please do not rush your process. Allow yourself to stay right where you are until you are ready to move on. Your spirit, your core soul, knows when to let go and get going. Listen to the signs and signals that your heart and soul are providing for you. That being said, don't stay longer than necessary. Do not suffer when it is time to close the chapter and move on. That is just as important as not moving until you are ready.

Finding ways to bring some form of normalcy back to the person's life is imperative. Setting energy in motion to bring back a feeling of *life* is equally as important. To think that we all mend, heal, and *forgive-and-forget* in the same time frame and with the same process is simply nonsense. Life is a personal experience. We have many types of energy attached to emotional and mental thoughts. There are many factors in how a person heals, moves forward, and creates a sense of balance in their life. It is very individual and must be allowed to be very individual by those supporting the environments of individuals healing and balancing themselves. That being said, we must all strive to "get back in the game" as quickly as it is truthfully possible.

How do we avoid challenges that emerge to disrupt this energy center? The reality, unfortunately, is that we cannot always escape the experiences necessary to grow as a human spirit. Change is inevitable. Life is change. Life is constantly moving. Even if we are not willing to participate in movement, those in our immediate circle, our community, our family, will, and do, continue to move through their life. We all participate in movement, and sometimes it is disrupting. That is the truth of life. Understanding options, making the best decisions for yourself, confirming your intention, and positioning yourself with the best attitude possible will assist you in handling the imperative changes and challenges. The ultimate goal for us all is to keep this energy center balanced. Constant monitoring and maintenance is a key.

For children of parents or caregivers who cannot fulfill their responsibility, consciously or unconsciously, knowingly or unknowingly, this energy center will need consistent attention. Children want and need their parents or caregivers to acknowledge and, hopefully, apologize for the pain and suffering they endured. Those who have felt trauma feel that they need to have confirmation for the pain and suffering that occurred. It's essential to many, not just children. Acknowledgment is powerful medicine. However, getting the acknowledgement from our parents or those who have hurt us is not always possible. Many people we will interact with in our life time must maintain their own "story line," e.g. "I did the best I could," even though the abuse was very apparent, to manage their existence. In essence, we may be on our own to resolve painful circumstances. Living in truth is painful at times. As we grow in years and experience, so will our understanding of life, those who are in it, and the connection to it all! Some of the most painful experiences can be of benefit later in life, as you will read from the stories in this book.

Keko's Story

In late 1999, I received a phone call about a young man who was having difficulty with many physical challenges. When Keko and I met, this young man had already undergone two major knee surgeries. His parents were wondering if he would be able to continue participating in sports, as he was a very active boy. He also suffered from insomnia. My immediate concern was helping him rest. This young man had not had a peaceful sleep in over 10 years. This was a serious challenge. The spirit of the young man could not find a place of comfort and so his physical body was unable to receive the nurturing, healing, and rejuvenation necessary to restore his system.

After several weeks of work, I realized that during the early days of his childhood he became severely stressed over the dynamics within his home. He had a broken family with a highly dysfunctional father and a mother who had "ego-blaming" based energy. She believed that it was everyone else's fault that her marriage was over and not working, instead of taking responsibility for herself. Sadly, she blamed her son's behavior for her husband's transgressions. She shifted her responsibility as a parent by not accepting accountability. His gentle energy accepted the responsibility of his mother's downfall, graciously, without confusion or conflict. He desperately wanted his family to *work*.

Keko came into this world with a uniquely different type of energy system than his mother. He was very empathetic to the point of storing all the events from his mother, father, and younger sister's life that hurts. When I looked into his system, I could see that he was carrying everyone else's pain. He transferred all of the pain, agony, sadness, and anger from his parents into his own energy system and body. The burden that this young man felt was incredible. There was no question in my mind that he was not able to sleep with all he worried about, stressed over, and accepted as his own challenges. I had never witnessed such a transference that is quite as severe.

This young man's energy was that of a 65 year old, the approximate age of his parents. The first part of our work was gentle. With absolutely no blame or reference to his parents, I wanted to help him see what was truly going on so he could understand that the energy he was carrying was not his responsibility. He needed to learn that his parents' pain was not his own. From the age of 3, this young man tried to *fix* and *mend* his father's addictions and his mother's anger and blame. The guilt he felt was beyond any emotional word I can use. The pain he felt in his heart was apparent each time we spoke. It was hard for him to hold back his tears, while his beautiful smile was still shining through during each and every session.

While we worked, Keko discovered that he had two massive hernias. He underwent another surgery to repair this immediate challenge. Again, it revolved around his lower extremities. Although he was doing his very best to overcome the challenges stemming from energy that was not his, his real self was also involved in the drama. The sadness and the anger of the broken family dynamics continued to weigh heavy in his heart and mind. Keko was no longer able to handle the stress of his family and his body showed it. His lower extremities were simply unable to carry the heavy weight of his family issues, pain, and conflict. His body began to slowly collapse. His Stability Energy Center was losing its strength and became seriously unbalanced.

Keko and I worked together to unwind his unhealthy connection with his family issues. Our desire was not to remove him from his family unit. Our goal was to move him into his own energy, supporting his own thoughts, dreams, and hopes. When he returned to playing the sport he loved, he once again felt pain. This time it was his foot that became severely damaged. His family searched and searched for the answers to the *new* condition. Nothing appeared on the CT or the MRI. This challenge lasted over a year. When a person is stuck inside themself, without the resources or understanding to move forward with confidence and clarity, the physical body will carry a sense of helplessnes--a feeling of internal despair without understanding the indication. As time went by and as Keko started working on his challenges alone, he began to wake up as he made more and more associations between the emotions of the *story* and his body's own interpretation and expression. He needed time to rethink how he would reunite and participate in a sport he loved

During his personal self-discovery period, he realized, understood, and *finally* accepted that he was not responsible for the damage that his parents inflicted on themselves and the family unit. Keko realized that he did not need to carry the blame nor did he need to fix what his parents created. Through his self-discovery and long, long hours of preparing for what he knew his future could be, he started to self-evolve. Started to understand the core strength he held within himself. The shift was incredibly solid and formed a foundation for him to embark on the future he was designing within his own structure--his own ideas, dreams and hopes!

Although the impact of his family's residue would never completely leave him, Keko took on the task of truly healing. The work he undertook to balance his life, his physical body, and his core spirit was not about *forgetting* or *forgiving*. It was not about burying the past. He simply understood that his responsibility as a young man did not include caring for, counseling, or holding space for his parents in the dynamic that was set up for him as a young boy. Keko was no longer the "keeper" of the family fall-out. He was a young man ready to only accept responsibility for his actions, dreams, goals, and his idea of life and how it would work out for him.

Through his many walks on the beach, hiking, swimming, and centering his energy on the earth, on a daily basis, Keko learned to stand on his own two feet--the two solid feet that were able to carry him into the next phase of his adult life. Today he lives a comfortable life in a place he loves and calls home. His body responds to joy, happiness, and the rhythm he has set for his life. He has taken his journey to a place he was unaware of many years ago. He now helps others who struggle with challenges within the mind, body, and spirit.

Creating Movement & Stability

RECONNECTING WITH YOUR STABILITY ENERGY

One of the biggest challenges of the Stability Energy Center is to clear energy that is not truly associated with your life path, your experiences, and your responsibility. When we give up a large part of ourselves in a moment to someone else, through an experience that was devastating, in a company or work situation, we can have *less than* what we need to secure our mind, body, and soul. Let's begin with truthful evaluation. When the burden of others is housed within ourselves, we can become weighted, frozen, and lose energy.

Grab your pen and pad. Sit in an area where you have no distractions. Turn your cell phone or any other communication devices off. It's not easy, I know. But for a moment, allow this time to be yours. Disconnect so you can reconnected!

Find the Root Cause: Breathe in and out slowly, with the intention to relax. The intention is crucial. Breathe into *what* the stability energy feels like for you. Focus on your Stability Energy Center. As you do so, visualize the color *red*.

Now:

- Write down 3 things about your life that need *immediate* attention.

- Write down 3 things in your life that you feel *overburdened* by.

- Write down 3 things that you feel you have carried or *shouldered* long enough.

Once you have determined the *root* cause of the instability of your life, there are necessary steps to create balance. To create stability, you must first believe that you are able to create stability. *Know you can.*

Create Balance

Here are some words of inspiration to help you create balance.

- Know that you want to change.

- Know that you are capable, at this very moment, of making small movement at your pace.

- Know that you are not responsible for the challenges, burdens, and pains of those around you.

- When being of service to others, make sure that you too are taken care of.

- Become aware of the energy that keeps you feeling unbalanced.

- Recognize when you must step away in order to create a platform for those you love to stand alone.

- Know that your connection to those around you must be of balanced and not of dependence.

- Feel the truth of what you need in order to keep your life on track. Know what your responsibility is.

- Know that not accepting responsibility for yourself is just as unbalanced as accepting too much.

Make a firm commitment to walk outside on the grass, sand, or dirt each and every day. Even though you believe that you don't have time, you truly do have the time for the things you find important. Have you ever noticed that we have time for things we don't want to do and never find the time for things we need or want? Rethink that!

Special Focus for Those Working on Financial Concerns:

Each day, when your financial worry energy comes to mind (and it will come to mind), please take a deep breath and repeat to yourself these empowerment phrases:

- My freedom is attached to allowing myself to let go of these thoughts.

- These fearful and negative thoughts are no longer necessary.

- I have confidence in my future.

- I am no longer afraid to let go of worry.

- There is nothing for me to attach my fear to.

- ☐ My success is a direct reflection of my ability to believe in myself.
- ☐ I am not afraid to move forward.
- ☐ I know my core self is with me every step of the day.
- ☐ I am not afraid to allow movement to take place.
- ☐ I am living my dream as I allow my internal knowledge to guide me.

Change can, and will, happen. If there are words from the above empowerment phrases that do not apply to you, or you do not feel the strength necessary to believe the words, please find your own. You know the truth! Do not allow fear to set the tone for your life. Hope and faith are two key words in making short and long term changes in life. You must believe that change is possible. It starts the seed within your own self. Knowing, or partially believing, is the next step necessary to create and feel the changes. You must recognize that you really are in charge.

Affirmations or words of empowerment will not shift energy without the firm belief of the participant. Unfortunately, this is a huge misconception in the world of *healing* and *self-help*. You must believe with all fibers within yourself that the change or shift is possible. Which means what you are saying must resonate with your energy--your belief system. Choose the words you need if the above phrases are not your style or feel believable. These phrases are meant to start your process!

Chapter 2.

THE PASSION ENERGY CENTER

Passion Energy

My body responds to goodness, joy, and happiness.

Significance: Creating joy, intimacy and enthusiasm for life. Sexual power. Family balance. Emotions attached to intimate relationships both sexually and intimately. Socializing comfortably. Wanting to feel and be touched. Embracing in creative activities that feel nice, warm, cozy, and give personal fulfillment and pleasure. Sharing oneself with others openly without restriction and reservation.

Balanced: We are tapped into high energy resources and have success in writing, creating, developing innovative business, interacting passionately with lover/spouse and creating a loving family. We feel joy and embrace life and the relationships we have brought in to support us.

Unbalanced: We can feel stagnation; we are unaffectionate, empty emotionally, and have a feeling of exhaustion, low energy, and inability to feel passion. Our connection to things that once brought us a feeling of satisfaction, happiness, and optimistic outlook has diminished dramatically or no longer exists. This energy center is a direct reflection of your intimate and sexual self. If you have insecurity in these areas, this area can easily become imbalanced with physical challenges. Kidney, prostate, and female organs can be a challenge of the Passion Energy Center.

෧๛෧෧෧෧෧෧෧෧෧

Passion energy is deeply associated with being alive. How important is passion in our lives? Without the feeling of passion, we tend to create an undeniable outlook of isolation, numbness, lifelessness, and disconnection with ourselves and those around us. This energy center is associated with our creativity and is associated with the genitals and reproductive areas of the body. When a person becomes indifferent within, areas of the physical body can become stagnant. Without passion, pleasure, or joy, we simply move through life and lack inner power, energy, or satisfaction. Passion is the vital energy behind our dreams and ideas and good health. It is also linked intrinsically to our thoughts and feelings.

Our physical, mental, and emotional body need and want to feel excitement, passion, creativity, and, above all, pleasure. Our mind, our mental self, must allow time for pleasure as well. Pleasure has many different meanings. It can describe what a person feels when they enjoy the sunset, take in a great concert, soak in the latest art exhibit, converse with a friend, cuddle with a pet or a child, or embrace your lover or spouse. It can be associated with the moment you pour bath salts into a warm tub after a long day of stressful activity. Whatever the association, pleasure is crucial and it is extremely important to balance the energy of life with this joyous energy.

We each interpret and embrace the idea of pleasure differently. And yes, there are many people who relate pleasure with sexual activity. This energy, during certain ages, has an enormous impact on the healthy hormones that run throughout our body. Sexual energy is a very powerful component in creating a sense of power. It is also a major power center for men. When I say *major*, I absolutely want to communicate without any misunderstanding the importance of this energy center for men-- it can create or destroy financial abundance as well as intimacy and relationships.

The Passion Energy Center represents different feelings for men and women. Women often relate this energy to affection, family, children, and components of safety and happiness. That is not to say that women don't want to be as sexual and sexy as men; many do. It is simply that some women protect this area of themselves by engaging in child bearing and then moving into the next phase of womanhood by nurturing a family environment. When this center is unbalanced for either men or women, it can set a chain of events in motion that affects all of the other energy centers. What does it feel like when you are in love or have the pure pleasure of engaging in an intimate sexual experience with someone you love and/or care for? How does it feel when you lose that connection? However it is that you engage in pleasurable activity, know that it is important to the overall well-being of the human self.

Without the emotions of pleasure and connectedness, we can experience the feeling of tiredness. Tiredness simply tells us that we do not have energy for anything other than what is necessary. It is a sign that life has become stale, boring, uninteresting, and without pleasure or joy. When the feeling associated with passion energy escapes you, knowingly or unknowingly, you can become withdrawn from your own curiosity and awe with life, as well as distant from events that once gave you a sense of happiness, joy, and excitement.

The truth is the very essence of why we keep pushing on with our dreams, ideas, thoughts, and daily lives is an attitude of optimism. The Passion Energy Center is the area of our physical body associated with a deep sense of how we feel within, how we feel about others, and how we feel about the future. This is where excitement, encouragement, and engagement with life reside.

What causes the feelings associated with passion, creativity, and joy to diminish or become unbalanced? There are many reasons why we can become displaced. Sudden changes in our life, a major disappointment, or an event that causes crushing emotional pain can cause big set-backs. So can financial fears, challenges with our children, and an environment that does not allow for creative expression. The greatest issues that feed imbalances within this energy center are disappointments associated with love, sexuality, family issues, and our lack of clarity about our personal intention as males and females. We can feel like the essence of our life force is threatened. That is because this energy center is associated with the male and female reproduction organs, the very essence of life's creation.

Finding Balance Within

Withholding energy from others when we are closely connected to them can be detrimental to everyone's well-being. Not communicating with those we need for support and love can create a deeper sense of despair. We need to function in life with passion, excitement, and hope for the future. Our children can, and do, hold an enormous amount of joyful energy. When we start to feel overwhelmed at the energy our children require, or what our lover or spouse requires, it is almost always due to what we lack in our own lives. We hold the key to giving them exactly what they want and need. Remember, we are all, each of us, engaged in the lives of those at this very moment for a reason. We bring each relationship to us for growth, love, understanding, and support. Do not misunderstand the energetic connection with those who you have surrounded yourself with.

When we are balanced within our own inner self, giving of ourself to those we love is a remarkable pleasure. It also gives us an enormous amount of energy. The exchange of giving and receiving is powerful for each person involved. The next time you are able to share yourself with someone, take a moment to see and feel the response. Loving, showing affection, and giving intimately to those we share our life with are efforts on our part at first. But when you allow this energy to flow freely from you to them, you will find even greater amount of energy becomes available to you.

How do you feel when you receive a hug or kiss from someone you love? How do you feel when someone acknowledges you? We, as human beings, want to be loved, acknowledged, touched, and cared for. We love to hear and feel the passion of ourself and those we love. Whether it comes naturally or we must make the effort to dig deep to find it. Then, dig deeper to create the confidence to use it. You will be amazed at the results.

Male Passion Energy

For men, the ability to create abundance and financial freedom is mainly associated with this energy center. This is where the male energy can become affected positively or negatively. Without a balance in this area of a male, the positive connection to finances can become challenged. He can accept and create the *victim* mentality towards finances or the feeling of not having enough even though there is plenty. Without passion and pleasure, it is difficult to maintain the energy to create abundance.

Financial abundance, associated with the male energy, is housed in this area of the physical body. Once this energy center has been damaged, become stagnant, or lost sensitivity, a male can become despondent in his connection to financial success and stability. His drive to see his vision as a reality can diminish.

Without creative flow of male energy through this system, a lifeless, unimaginative, and complacent energy will appear. Sometimes, this numbness can flip energetically into expressions of frustration or violence. It might be aimed inward and become self-sabotaging behavior, or shoot outward and become destructive to others.

Male success, male energy, and male ego are tied to this energy center. When a male is satisfied within this area of himself sexually, he is not restless, indecisive, or complacent. He is empowered by his own strength. A sexually satisfied male is a male with an enormous amount of innate internal power. His vision is typically strong and concise and the other areas of his life are normally in balance. A male without balance in this area can be flat, detached, and lifeless, or he can develop a pattern of self-indulgence. If a male is connected or bound, due to family responsibility, to a female who has extremely strong and direct energy, without a strong emotional connection, the male can feel weak and his Passion Energy Center can become weak and a breeding ground for health challenges.

What Created an Imbalance In the Passion Energy Center:

- Sudden shock or realization attached to love, affection, or being in a relationship.
- Realizing that a feeling of *falling in love* was truly a *lust* feeling.

- A woman not returning to normal hormone function after childbirth. A male losing his job or source of income.

- A male finding he is over his head with responsibilities he is unprepared to handle successfully.

- A woman realizing that her life suddenly, even though it's been years, has too many household and domestic responsibilities.

- A male feeling his masculine energy has been damaged by a strong woman's energy.

- A male feeling he is a source of *income* for his family or wife.

- A woman overwhelmed with a career and her family responsibilities.

- A male or female suddenly faced with single parenting.

- A male or female facing, entering, or after a divorce.

- A woman losing her ability to control her personal intimate self and the demands of her life.

- A parent feeling they have let their family down.

- On-going dysfunctional energy inside a home environment without resolve.

- Numbness created by a sense of failure in relationship, career, or family.

These are a few challenges that can create a feeling of imbalance in the Passion Energy Center. We are all in this moment of life together. We can reach out at any time. Checking in with those in our life is very important. Allowing the process of healing, without restrictions or time lines, to occur naturally within ourselves and those in our life is the key. Being acknowledged during our moments of pain and uncertainty can be just what we need to get back on track. Acknowledgment and compassionate support is one of the fundamentals of sharing love!

Karina's Story

In 1990, I began work with a woman who had developed uterine cancer. She had been notified through her physician that her cancer had spread to stage three. During our first meeting, I pulled out a set of tools I like to use: identification cards associated with the energy centers. Without reading any of the writing on the cards, I asked her to select the card associated with the greatest imbalance she felt in her life at that moment. She immediately picked up the card associated with passion energy.

It has been my experience, working with individuals who feel imbalance in their mind, body, or spirit, that they themselves hold the key to understanding the problem and often the ability to rebalance it within themselves. The identifying cards I developed are tools I use to encourage the wisdom of the participant in finding their own answers to their challenges. With their keen insight, they are able to discover more about their challenges than they originally thought possible. It is a tool that has created a sense of empowerment for those seeking an understanding that can lead to their own growth and healing. When the individual is able to unconsciously or consciously meet me at the door of the underlying reason for the illness, creating a plan can be easy and change can be rapid.

Karina knew deep inside why she was instrumental in creating the imbalance in the female organ area. She was tired, worn out, confused, and exhausted. When she married her husband just after high school, they both had high hopes for the future. During the first 6 years, her husband had moved the family around quite a bit because of work. Having two children, at the age of 25, created an inner struggle in Karina, who also had her own childhood taken from her as abuse ran in her family. She had never experienced the pleasures and happiness associated with a stable childhood.

Now, as an adult, she was responsible for two children who desperately needed all the energy she had from the moment she woke up to the moment she passed out at night. She was not enjoying the pleasures of motherhood and felt disconnected from the outside world. Karina was also totally discombobulated in the world inside her home and, most importantly, her inner self. Her experience, within her own thought process, was interpreted as feeling abandoned--all alone without support from her husband. She never felt that he had the same challenges since he had a job, colleagues, and entertainment associated with his career. Karina felt helpless most days, living inside a home she sensed was empty and without happiness. The struggle of raising two children on her own (even though her husband was home every night) was too much pressure. She felt anxious and started smoking marijuana while taking anti-depressants for relief.

Self-medication led to many new challenges. The schedule she once had no longer existed. The meals were not prepared for her children on time. She became so tired that she stopped cooking altogether. She started to purchase frozen food that she could pop into the microwave. She and her husband began fighting. He did not want his children eating fast food nor did he appreciate seeing her untidy on a regular basis. He became very disenchanted with his wife's outlook. He did not feel that she was stable.

Karina's husband had a childhood quite different from hers. His mother and father were not divorced and they had set roles. His mother stayed home with the children and his father had a career. His mother volunteered in the community and kept house. Karina had no idea of what this lifestyle looked like or how to interact within it. She knew that she was not the type of wife or mother her husband required or expected. Although she knew her short-comings going into the relationship years ago, she hoped that she might be able, with time, to grow into the person he wanted her to be--and--the woman and mother she wanted to be. She did not want the confusion or unsettling issues associated with her own childhood to happen inside her own home. But it was not possible. Karina did not have the life skills to fit into this environment as quickly as was needed.

Shortly after the marriage ceremony, the children arrived, which they both agreed on. They were both very excited to start their family. Danny's idea of *family* and Karina's idea, they later found, was the difference between the color of black and white.

Before coming up for any air, two children later, Karina felt a continuous displacement, due to several relocations. This did not allow for the learning curve she needed to settle into the natural family lifestyle her husband had created. After this honest evaluation of just where her life was, she started to neglect her hair and her clothing choices. She was no longer interested in taking care of herself as she had years before. It was no longer a priority. She described it this way: "It's everything for me to remember to get three meals a day for my children. I don't have time to think about myself anymore."

Although she tried on numerous occasions to speak to her husband about her severe challenges, he was not able to hear her. He was too busy creating income to sustain the family. Her husband did not grow up in a family where the mother discussed her intimate challenges. Instead, his mom was the foundation that allowed his father to maintain his status in society. But, Karina was not Danny's mother. He was more and more disappointed in her and his days became longer and longer at the office. The weekends started to blend into his work days. He totally disconnected from his family. During their 8th year of marriage, her husband started an affair with a woman from the office. He felt he needed to create some type of balance within his own life to maintain the family responsibilities he knew he was accountable for. The energy inside his home was too much for him to handle. He wanted to run away. When Karina found out about the other woman, she was devastated. That was the last straw. The illusion of her marriage and her life as a mother came crashing down.

Within 6 months, she was in the office of her physician complaining of heavy pain and abnormal bleeding. The CT showed a uterus completely covered in tumors. His advice was surgery and chemo therapy. When she delivered the news during our appointment, I sat with her and gazed into her eyes. I wanted to know energetically which road she would take on this part of her journey--would she let go from exhaustion and fear of the future or fight for herself and her children? When illness sets into the physical body, it can have a profound effect on the emotional self. Depending upon the immune system and the emotional system, choices are made on many levels of a human psyche. Conscious and unconscious choices are made. The spirit of oneself can come into and develop a powerful position.

The energy of illness can hold a great deal of past memory association. We held hands as she talked about what life meant to her and what it might mean to her children if she were no longer here to love and support them. With this news, her children became the focus of her life. She needed to come up with answers to who would care for her children and how, if she was not available. Suddenly, almost shockingly, Karina found her voice. In her mind and in her heart, her two children now became the joy and love/heart focus of her day. She had always felt this connection but felt disconnected from herself. Now, from that point forward, they were a team. They were in this fight together.

Healing is a process. The teacher, doctor, or advisor can only take you so far. You will have the energy inside to push on, or you will not. Depending on how far your illness has taken you, at times the immune system might not be able to make it back to normal. This is a core reason to listen to your body. Listen to the signs and signals it gives you! Karina's decision to push through required her to take a hard look at her life. She needed to really find out what she had within herself as a young woman, regardless of her childhood. She needed to reconnect to her inner strength and realize what her priorities were and what she was able to do to create a place for healing within the walls of her current environment. With the help of her two sons, who loved her deeply and needed her companionship and guidance immensely, Karina made the decision to undergo surgery. With or without the support of her husband, she had two beautiful smiling faces greeting her each day with love and compassion, with a phrase she heard often: "Mommy, you can do it." She started to believe it within herself. Grabbed onto that energy, stuffed it into her heart area, and held on with dear life.

Karina had to embrace and acknowledge the experiences that were so painful for her in childhood: her mother leaving her abusive father, living without the means to support a family as a single mother, and the hardship that endured because of those decisions. For once, the memories were a blessing. She realized that watching her mother endure the hardship year-after-year gave her the foundation to rebuild her own life with her two children. An experience she never felt could provide her with anything but pain was now the cornerstone that would help her move forward with her own life.

Checking in with her months after the surgery, I was happy to hear that the changes she made in her life allowed her more stability than she had ever thought possible. Karina realized that even though we have had painful moments in our life and our childhood, our future is not determined by our past. Rather, it is determined by the energy we put into our daily life. Today, Karina lives with a great sense of hope and self-confidence. She lives with the encouragement that life can continue to be a wonderful experience regardless of where you are or where you come from. She understands today that painful and unhappy moments in childhood can, and did, come to her aide. She also understood that the fear, sadness, and despair when viewing from a very different perspective than the one she had formed as a child allowed her to persevere with the knowledge that there is light at the end of the tunnel, regardless of how dark (and how long it has been) the tunnel is.

Creating Pleasure & Joy

RECONNECTING WITH YOUR PASSION ENERGY

This major energy center requires consistent monitoring to keep it flowing. Here are some simple activities to support your passion energy. Be as honest as you can with yourself. You are alone. No one is listening, no one is monitoring you. Allow these moments to be yours, without judgment or question. Feel free to answer out loud or write your answers down in a journal.

To Begin: Breathe fresh air deep into your lungs 3 times slowly. Clear the clutter and noise associated with the moment of your day. Be with yourself for just a moment. Just yourself.

To Connect: Here are four questions that will help to acknowledge the energy associated with the attachment to this energy center. The important part of this exercise is to *hear, feel, and acknowledge* what is being given to you for support. If you feel your way through the exercise, you will also be connecting to your Intuitive Energy. This connection will become very important as you start to balance the energy centers. Ready to listen to your inner self? Breathe deep, let's go!

☐ What does true passion feel like for me?

- Where I am right now in my life, what can I instantly bring to myself to get the feeling of passion, fun, life, and excitement to me?
- What do I need to eliminate to make room for the time I need to embrace life?
- What am I willing to do to get the process of reconnection going?

Repeat these questions daily for a week. As you remind yourself what your passion is, you will strengthen the awareness and power within the Passion Energy Center. Listen to your body's language. Feel your body's request, your body's desires. Don't forget to put your words into action. Slowly or quickly, just make sure you put action to your words of what passion feels like today. It can be as simple as a cup of tea or coffee by yourself or with a friend. A 5-minute phone call with someone you are close to, a night out with the guys, or a bath with no interruptions. We are all different in our needs to bring happiness, joy, and pleasure back into our lives. Of course, it can even be engaging intimately the way it *used* to be or the way you thought it might have been before all the responsibilities of life set in. Make time to reconnect to the Energy of Life!

As you walk through your day, be mindful to see and feel experiences that will ignite your passionate self. Look for it. When you see or engage in something playful, exciting, and fun, acknowledge it. Right then, acknowledge that you are feeling and sensing feelings of excitement. The increase of awareness through the confirmation as often as possible strengthens and empowers this extremely important energy center.

Reconnect With Yourself

When you balance your inner self, you will extend and provide that energy to others. Without it circulating within, it cannot be given outwardly. If you are one of us who extend, extend, and extend because of duty and project out that you *did your very best* even though you are exhausted, frustrated, and running on empty, let me share this with you: the energy you are using because of responsibility thoughts is making the situation worse.

Stretching yourself out of responsibility without first taking care yourself will not, and can not, have a 'real' benefit to anyone.

People who love you want to feel your *love* energy. How possible is it to truly extend *love* energy when you are exhausted? We must start with the truth of the energy we hold right now. Right this minute. If we are rushed, running behind the bus, slamming coffee, and still coming up short, so be it. That is where we start.

When our passion or creative energy starts to dim, dig deep to find the reasons that life or the feeling of life has changed for you. When you start to disconnect from things in your life that once created a feeling of joy, happiness, and satisfaction, take time to reconnect with yourself. Creating awareness is the key. Living with truth is important. Even if you do not admit it to anyone but yourself, face the challenges you feel head on. Do not make the mistake of pushing yourself to create what was lost or at times taken from you. Take the necessary steps, even if they are baby steps, to recreate what you know is possible and what you know is comfortable. Remember that you want passion, want creativity, and want to have fun! You want to feel the upside of life, don't you?

Please be mindful: if you have someone in your life who starts to disconnect from the usual outlets used for enjoyment and pleasure, take a moment to communicate with him or her. When the energy shift is caught early on, it is not so difficult to get back to a place of balance. Often times, it simply takes a little acknowledgment--the awareness that something painful or disarming has occurred, and someone cares.

Remember to take the time to care for yourself and create the opportunities you need as an individual to keep your body in balance. To implement, regardless of your schedule, the time necessary to enjoy a moment each day is extremely important to your overall well-being. Know this! Even if it is a moment, do it! Find and engage in the pleasures that were and are important to you. I know it is often impossible, truly impossible, to remember what that feeling is when you have been through so many stressful times. But, *try*. Put effort into this. Even 5 minutes a day will start the journey you need to make a shift.

Enhance Your Passion Center with Gentle Movements

I want you to know that your body wants to be alive. It wants to feel. It wants to engage in feelings of excitement or enthusiasm. Your emotional, physical, and mental self want to participate and be active. The hips, lower back, and pelvic area all need movement. It is the core of where energy can move forward and backward, upward and downward. Feel those words for a moment. This part of the body requires movement to breathe internally and externally. Stagnation can create great pain in areas that we are most vulnerable for both men and women. Let's get ready to get the energy shaking and moving. Move at your own pace. This is not an exercise. It's a movement to awake dormant and stagnant energy flow.

Rock your body from front to back using your hips. Take a breath in and move your pelvic area up front, breathe out while you are rocking your pelvic area to the back. Do not stress your body--this is gentle movement. You can put on some of your favorite music. It will gently move the vibration of the body as you move. You can also tap three times on the area just below your belly button. When you commit yourself to this movement at least 2 times a day, you will find your Passion Energy Center coming back to life with balance and with great depth. If you remember the answers to the questions you just answered, you can affirm the words as you move through this energy movement. If you've turned on the music, find your groove. Move this area of your body to your own personal rhythm. Remember, no one is listening or watching! Have fun....

Chapter 3.

The Self Assurance Energy Center

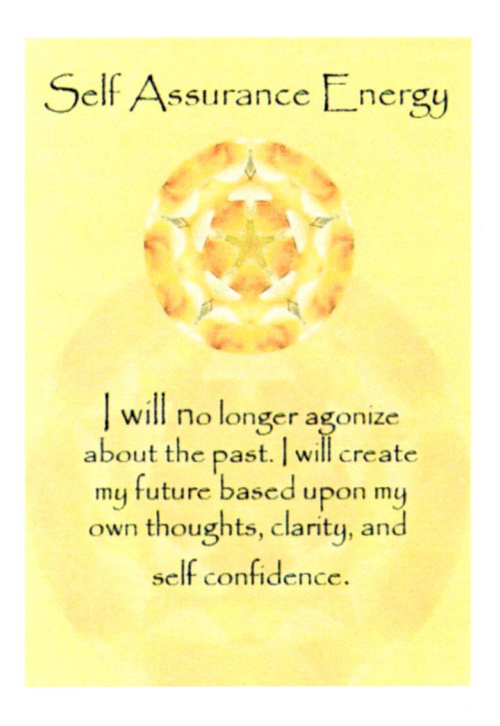

Self Assurance Energy

I will no longer agonize about the past. I will create my future based upon my own thoughts, clarity, and self confidence.

Significance: Confidence without ego and arrogance. Clarity in decision making. Feeling of compassion and patience with self and others. No need to dwell on past emotions. Knowing internal strength relating to self. Understanding the internal power we have. Not utilizing ego power. Knowing experiences have appeared to assist us with growth.

Balanced: We feel the confidence to create, implement a plan of action, and achieve goals that we have set in social, personal, and professional circumstance. Feeling a sense of accomplishment, association, and overall comfort with interaction internally and externally. A person who is not selfish, a person who can give without expectation and without wanting. A person who is compassionate with their feelings of others.

Unbalanced: We can feel frustrated, angry, and argumentative. Feelings of not being good enough or having enough. A feeling of distress in social settings, professional interaction, and personal affiliations. Feelings of being left out or disconnected from the dreams, ideas, and goals you have set. A feeling of distress in all circumstances: despair, anxiousness, over worry, over thinking, uncomfortable within oneself. Eating disorders, under and over eating. Creating challenges with food and the assimilation of nutrients and minerals needed to process life's energy. Liver function that becomes stagnant, inflamed, and sluggish can be a challenge of the self-assurance energy.

҈҈҈҈҈҈

Self-assurance energy is about how you interpret the world, how you are seen in the world, how you interact in the world personally, and how you want to be seen in the world. It is the energetic center associated with believing in one's self, future, and the ability to reach goals and live dreams. Self-assurance energy revolves around confidence and the ability to see and feel the possibility of manifesting one's desires. Life is filled with challenges. Without self-assurance energy, our connection to our inner self: our dreams, goals, and ideas may be weak or nonexistent and it will be difficult to get things done. Self-assurance energy is deeply tied to personal power as well as inner core strength and resolve. It is very important to us and involves the confidence in how we interact with others, our careers, and the big picture of our lives. It is ultimately the connection we have with our inner self, and how we see ourselves in the world.

How do we lose and regain self-assurance? Where does self-confidence come from? Is it taught or felt? How do we interact in life when we feel self-confident, content with our choices and our decisions? How do we live life when our self-confidence and self-esteem is compromised? Or, as we grow within the frame of life, how we take responsibility as adults when our self-confidence was pulled away! What happens when intentional violation occurs to the vulnerable? The loss and the fragmented pieces of their self-assurance energy can dissicpate to the point of total malfunction and disfunction.

What happens when we give away or someone takes away our self-esteem/self-assurance? What happens when we ignore our own insight and inner wisdom?

> *When we feel or intellectually believe that a person or opportunity holds more wisdom or value than what we can create within ourselves, that is, we have given our own power away.*

Living a life without self-assurance and self-confidence can lead to frustration, anger, internal digestive challenges, and, most importantly, weight issues--from being underweight due to nervousness and anxiety to overweight due to metabolism challenges associated with emotions and hormone fluctuation. One of the first indications of imbalance in this energy center can be digestion challenges. You may find yourself unable to process nutrients. You may always feel tired, nervous, anxious, unhappy, or powerless. Another indication is anger and frustration. Always feeling life is not fair or *right*. Not being able to get things straight or moving forward as you believe you should. And you may find that you are always looking outside yourself for answers when you know, on some level, the information you need lies within.

So often, we fail to listen to our inner instinct, our *guts*, even though we know better. When was the last time you knew the truth, your personal feeling of the truth, regardless of the circumstances, but you did not act accordingly? When was the last time you knew that you shouldn't have made the choice you made, but, in some deep self-sabotaging way, you made it anyway? When you cultivate your self-assurance energy, you can change the energy associated with hesitation and confusion. It is the beginning of empowering yourself with your own self-knowledge. To start the connection with self-assurance energy, it is important that you:

- Believe in your personal choices, all of your choices, *regardless of the outcome or result*. Know that each decision brought you closer to understanding yourself.

- Believe you have the answers within yourself. Your core has the answer.

- Have the courage to speak up for yourself, speaking your confident truth.

- Know that the decisions and choices you are making are personal and are exactly what your spirit/core self needs. *Do not* second guess your first impulse.

- Find alignment and security with all decisions you make. *Own them!*

This journey is not only about making decisions that outwardly seem *right*. This journey is about making choices and decisions that help with us understanding ourselves and the growth of the human spirit.

Our inner self, our self-confidence, knows right and wrong in relation to the circumstances in our life. Remember, this is energy, a vessel that can assist us in preserving our inner knowing. The stomach area is the physical area where this self-assurance energy resides. Let's look at an example of how the stomach or self-assurance energy assists us or alerts us.

When you are preparing to speak to someone or you are in the midst of speaking to someone, what happens when you become aware that you are uncomfortable? Normally, you will instinctively raise one or both arms and cross them over the stomach area. Until you have established a level of comfort or self-assurance, you will remain with your arms enclosing your stomach area, just below the breast bones. Why? Why do we automatically raise up our arms to protect ourselves, our self-assurance area? Because we are assessing the situation. We are protecting ourselves from something that was or is being said that we feel uncomfortable about, or we are protecting and shielding ourselves from that person. The next time you start to feel uncomfortable with a situation, a person, or a relationship, be aware of your body language. Also be aware of the other person's body language if you might make them feel uncomfortable.

How Our Self-Assurance Energy Changes in Our Lives

What happens to our self-esteem? How does it become challenged or weakened in our lifetime? As children, we engage in relationships with our family that encourages self-confidence and self-assurance, or we do not. It is very simple. We are in an environment that teaches us through words or actions that we are special, lovable, capable, and have the ability to succeed, or we do not.

If a child grows up with constant ridicule, this child may have challenges believing in themself, regardless of the circumstances. If a child was unable to make choices and decisions or did not gain praise or rewards for tasks well done, or even words of praise and excitement, they may not have the opportunity to gain self-confidence and self-assurance growing up. They may even experience an empty or uneasy feeling in their bellies, the area associated with self-assurance energy. When you are not acknowledged for your efforts, regardless of the task, you start to lose the connection to what you might have gained in your self-assurance area. After years of not being acknowledged, you may feel nervous, anxious, or fiddling while trying to concentrate and yet not be able to connect to that comfort feeling of having the core confidence knowing.

As adults, overcoming the emotional and mental challenges we endured during childhood can be challenging, painstaking, and often unbearable. Until we mature into understanding what life experience can bring to us as strong support, we at times feel helpless to reconnect or create a sense of self-knowing. These life experiences become our valuable resource that if we cut ourselves off from them, we suffer. Living without self-confidence, self-esteem, and self-assurance can be crippling. Most of us will spend our entire 20's and 30's creating, through various opportunities, some sense of self-assurance and self-esteem. It is a process that can create a sense of exhilaration, joy, excitement, and fun. What a difference it makes to have strength in this area after a childhood without. This is a great sense of personal accomplishment. Developing and maintaining it is of the upmost importance.

Sometimes though, adults who are successful in their lives can lose their edge and self-esteem. What can suddenly take you so off-balance that it can be difficult, or perhaps is not achievable, to get back to the place you once lived within your life? Vulnerability! When we open ourselves to a circumstance, a person, a relationship, or an opportunity where we feel confidence, stability, future purpose, and comfort, but without the outcome we anticipated; or an experience we were not prepared for creeps in, making us feel raw or almost naked. Depending upon the particulars, the shock or discomfort can be unbearable, stripping a person of everything they believed they had and were made of. This type of experience can be the breeding ground for illness and dis-ease. It is one of the most common challenges in the health and wellness industry: the journey back to "oneself."

The Mental Self vs. the Emotional Self

The mind is filled with thoughts. It can become a kind of echo that loops what you have fed into it back to you, over and over and over again. These thoughts then gain strength, impact, and believability, even if they are not true! The mind is a mechanism; *it is only a mechanism*. The mind does not have emotion, but it has control over the contents kept in a storage area along with the associated emotions. For example, a song, a moment of recollection, or a word that has been instilled is a part of the *accessing* procedure that triggers our emotions. If we hear a song that is dear to us, our emotions will flood. Our buttons have been pushed, our heart races, our blood pressure can go up, our body can start to sweat, and all sensations are activated! Great memories, sad memories, memories with enthusiasm, memories of hope, etc. They can all be accessed with the tune of a song, whether it was stored from long, long ago or just last week. Fascinating, isn't it?

Why do these emotions flood? Does our mind feel? Did our *mind* feel that moment? No, our mind does not feel. It simply retrieves the information you stored in relation to the emotion or feelings or moments you felt while listening to that song. So, in reality, the mind does nothing more than *access* that experience you stored, thus allowing it to attach itself to that memory and moment. Mind is then attached to emotion. I believe that an emotion can be accessed through triggers, buttons, and "land mines" that are accessed, as stored information, by the mind. So if we know the mind does not feel, we can then look at the disturbance from an emotional perspective. We can become aware of what triggers the experience.

When we are burdened by the experiences and moments of destruction, abuse, and unhealthy lifestyles from the past, we cannot live in the present moment; we are dragging energy that does not allow for newness, progress, health, or happiness. What happens to us? What happens to the person we were? What happens to the knowing inside that can guide our life in the direction of a balanced self and enjoying who we are? Our past dictates our future. Thoughts today are tomorrow's reality. Energy of the past, unless it is processed properly, can lead to self-destruction and suffering.

The dilemma lies when we feel or made to believe that we are responsible to forgive those who treated us poorly-- intentionally discredited our spirit or soul self. I am a firm believer that we do not forget or forgive and then everything is ok. My personal belief is that we must focus on rebuilding our core inner strength, rather than the process of forgiving others. Throughout the years of my private practice, I have sat with the individuals who have struggle emotionally and mentally with the idea of obtaining complete closure or conclusion with those they must forgive, somehow believing that forgiveness is the ticket to their freedom.

For those who can not reach satisfactory concludion with forgiveness, there is a component within the self-confident/self-esteem energy that is in conflict with that past story. It is my opinion and belief that true freedom, mentally or emotionally, come as you focus on your inner core strength without the need to concern over those who engage in the imbalance. Please allow yourself to focus on rebuilding your inner strength. We can simply allow god or creator to engage in forgiveness or whatever is necessary, allowing us to move foreward without that responsibility.

The greatest gift you can give yourself is to gain or regain self-assurance energy. Over time, you will find that it fills your soul and allows you to share yourself more with others. It will also draw people to you and give you access to new positive, powerful experiences as well as an opportunity to tap into infinite energy.

Meredith's Story

Meredith came into my office complaining of stomach problems. She was often unable to hold down food. She no longer enjoyed eating. Every time she finished a meal, she felt anxiety. She bloated and suffered indigestion. She was experiencing a slowdown of her digestion, and a *gripping* sensation in her gut area made her feel uneasy and out of control. She also often felt severe pain lodging in her left upper stomach cavity, just under the rib cage.

Meredith was also exhausted, had panic issues, and was not able to get through her day without crying. We sat for a few hours discussing her uncomfortable symptoms and the issues that were upsetting her. As an experienced intuitive, it is important at times to allow the person to communicate what they feel the *real* issues are, even though it may or may not be the clear version. Truth is a very tricky word, especially when you tie in emotion, mental uneasiness, and the person's need to believe the truth as they tell it. Unfortunately, we can all create *stories* to help with how we feel. Although the stories are not always in direct conflict with the real truth, they can at times have added experiences or feelings that can complicate the truth.

As I sat and listened, I watched her hold her stomach with both hands. She was very upset with her husband, her daughter, her ex-husband, and the friends she had recently developed friendships with. She constantly referred back to "better times" when her life was filled with great experiences and feelings of happiness and contentment. Those were the days she did not fret or stress over trivial issues.

We discussed her blessed life from twenty years earlier and she became very excited. She did not hold her stomach during those conversations and I noted how she talked with zest and great energy. I realized she felt that her life only truly existed in the past and was not alive for her in the present. She was unable to embrace anything going on today. Something had happened that stopped her in her tracks and she could not step into life as it unfolded from that significant day on.

Several years back, Meredith had high hopes for a new and second marriage. Although she had felt a bit of intuition telling her that it was not the best move, particularly for her two children, she got married again anyway. She wanted to believe it was going to all work out for the best, for each of them. After being alone for eight years, she felt the courage she needed to embark on another marriage, after her husband's death. The years she had been married had brought great joy and happiness to her and her family. At the time, she was not responsible for having a career or financial stability. She was a mother and a loving wife. The pride she felt as she moved through her life and moments with her family sustained her very soul. She knew how to support her children in a loving and carefree manner while gently supporting, caring, and loving her husband. Her world revolved around loving and supporting those she cared for.

After her husband's untimely death, she felt a need within herself to open the door to the possibility of uniting with another man. She did not want her children to live without a father figure nor did she want to live without a life partner. The fifteen years she spent with her first husband only held wonderful memories for her and her children.

She was introduced to a man she felt would be a wonderful husband as well as a great father. Her responsibility as a mother was something she did not take lightly. Although, over the years, she had opportunities to meet with possible partners, she had not felt that she was ready until the day she met Sam. There was something about Sam that created a sense of excitement that she had not felt since the passing of her husband. Sam, too, had been married once, years ago. There were no children from the marriage. After a few dinners and several evenings of discussions, the couple decided to embark on a life together as a family. A marriage was planned! Meredith was filled with hope for herself and her children. If the next twenty years were like the past, this family unit was headed for wonderful times.

When the children met with Sam, initially and on several later occasions, both the daughter and son had a feeling of uneasiness. They voiced their opinion to their mother. They both felt that Sam was not being his true self. Although they could not describe it in words, the daughter did say, "Mom, he's hiding something." Meredith listened politely while she tried to uncover the real reason for the uncomfortable feelings they both had experienced. During her time with Sam, she did not see him as anything but generous, kind, and thoughtful.

Normally, she would have listened to her children. But under these circumstances, the passing of her husband and being alone for several years without his loving comfort and shoulder to lean on, she felt that she needed outside support to reach a decision on this very serious subject. She saw an advisor who told her that the children were suffering from separation anxiety and may not be open to allowing another man outside of their father to enter their lives. The advisor encouraged her to accept the marriage proposal for herself and her children.

During the weeks that led up to the wedding, little signals popped up that made Meredith uncomfortable. During an evening out in town, Sam drank more than usual. He became irritable with the waiter and raised his voice while discussing issues surrounding the children. He quickly caught himself and apologized. His excuse was the tension he felt surrounding the marriage, relocation of his belongings, and the expense of the wedding. He finally started to open up and voice his opinions about the future and his fears. While Meredith listened, she felt uneasy and agitated. She doubted her decision to marry Sam. She felt as though she needed to pull back and re-evaluate the relationship.

The following day she called her advisor. He told Meredith that he felt her fears were unfounded, that she was getting cold feet. She was assured that within a few months' time the family would blend nicely together, embarking on a new adventure.

Several days prior to the wedding day, family started to arrive. Meredith heard the opinions of family members as they began to meet and interact with Sam. Some liked and accepted him, but Meredith's mother in particular did not like him at all and sensed that he was hiding his true personality. Meredith chose to move forward. A decision she accepted full responsibility for. She heard opinions and made the choice to move forward regardless of the signs and signals that were being shown to her. Choosing to ignore her inner feelings, her personal knowing, changed the course of her life--the life she knew and felt comfort within.

The day of the wedding, Sam was drunk. Meredith was horrified and surprised. The honeymoon was also not as she expected. She felt empty and isolated instead of loving and intimate. Sam's intoxication did not allow for any intimacy. What had she done? Although all the feelings surrounding the initial connection and attraction to Sam were still there, signs of difference and dysfunction started to arise.

A few months into the marriage, the children started to speak less, retreating into their separate rooms. The relationship with their new step-dad did not unfold the way they had hoped or expected. Slowly, the family unit started to shut down. Life, as these 3 individuals knew it, was over. Sam also started to shut down. Although he wanted to be the father and husband Meredith and her children longed for, it was not possible.

Sam did not like noise. His version of what noise meant was not apparent initially. As time went by, the "children's voices and needs" became "noise." Although this was not communicated at first, it was real. Sam did not want to face the reality of how he had lived his life the past ten years, or twenty years for that matter. In his mid 40's, there were many challenges he faced by uniting with this or any family unit. Many of the reasons that his first marriage ended in divorce were slowly becoming alive again. Meredith did her very best to keep the lid on the volatile situation. But, soon after the marriage, the yelling began, as did the excessive drinking and the abusive language.

The incident that created the total collapse of Meredith's sense of self, her sense of pride and self-confidence, was the day Sam shoved Megan against the wall when she raised her voice expressing anger and rage about the interaction he displayed with her mother. The result of the hostile moment was the point of no return. The three years following were felt through a state of numbness. The children had no one to turn.

During the years of trying to get out of the marriage, with no energy, no self-esteem, and no confidence, the children were set to the side with their needs. She could not find the strength or insight to help either of them successfully. Finally, a personal friend stepped in to extend financial help and emotional support to get the ball rolling on the inevitable divorce process. This once very content and happy family had turned into three human beings desperately holding onto whatever they had in the past as a kind of false sense of security and stability on a day-to-day basis. Each living in the past, desperately grabbing for comfort that was not in reach, not being able to see clearly the future or feel any sense of balance.

Three years later, Meredith sits in front of me repeating the same *story* as she tries to remain alive in the past, unable to move forward with any sense of self-assurance. She spent two years trying to find herself again. Although Meredith had the self-confidence to make sound decisions from an early age, the relationship and interaction with Sam, and her unwillingness to listen to her own gut feelings that things were never right, disconnected her from her own self-assurance and self-confidence. Her body was expressing its pain and distress in her center of power, right in her stomach. Each time she looked at her children, the once very happy and content loves of her life-- now sitting looking lifeless and without calm expression, the pain got worse. It was even worse when she started to think of the past, remembering the wonderful times that were no more.

After the divorce, Meredith spent a few years in self-discovery. Her children were able to feel the essence of their mother again, although not exactly the same as their childhood memories. Returning to the close family unit they all needed, the foundation was now being built on a platform very different from what they had experienced in the past. The children were older now. Their individual life experiences were instrumental in building the foundation that they now live from. With Meredith at the helm, listening and engaging with her children as she so sadly missed helped her regain her self-assurance. Rebuilding a strong family unit, with many life lessons to express to each other, is undertaken within this strong family bond.

In order to bring Meredith back to reclaim her self-assurance, I developed a series of exercises to help her to change her patterns, step-by-step, day-by-day. I asked her to keep a journal of her thoughts and her feelings. I also suggested that three times a day she read her empowerment phrases out loud, into a mirror. Eye to eye contact. In addition, I encouraged her to alter her daily life plans, little by little, with a strong intention to reclaim her self-assurance and desire, with the promise that through her commitment she would build the energy to support, and start to feel, her personal goals being realized.

Meredith suggested some of her daily changes would include a slow walk in nature, conversations that were mostly upbeat, and the deep conviction that negative self-talk would be stopped as soon as she identified it as such. Walking clears the mind and gives the physical body a moment to oxygenate. Upbeat conversations provide energetic connection to positive interaction. Her self-awareness of the unhealthy chatter--allowing it to have only a moment in the mind, sifting through what is no longer necessary, and then repeating the mantra of why that *noise* is no longer necessary--is a strong medicine.

Creating Self-Confidence

RECONNECTING WITH YOUR SELF-ASSURANCE ENERGY

How do we regain ourselves? How do we regain our connection to our spirit, the spirit of who we truly are?

The following exercises are what I developed to help us reconnect with ourself. They build the muscles that help you know who you really are and support you as you embrace the task of making your own self-assured decisions.

Changing Your Pattern: 4 Steps

1. Awareness. Become aware of the signs, feelings, sensations, body clues, and thoughts that bring you into negativity, which is the state you want to avoid. This negativity could be formed in two different ways:

1a. Signs, feelings, sensations, and body clues associated with the gut feeling. You will want to look for and acknowledge the followings: nervousness in the stomach area, a feeling of wanting to raise your arm and guard your stomach or chest, a feeling of warmth of heat that comes across any area of your body, your mental challenge to find answers, or the simplest unbalanced feeling when engage in conversation, physical contact, opportunities, or developing relationship with others. If you ignore these gut intelligences, if you refrain or refuse to acknowledge and conclude these sensations repeatedly, this will be the plateform and magnet leading to difficulties in your life.

1b. Negative thinking pattern. The emotional engagement with negative thinking can be debilitating. Our thought, each and every thought, will run through our physical energy system. When we think of happy thought, thoughts of hope and empowerment, our body responses flavorably. Our body, our physical self, will need additional assurance/resources when we continually attach ourself to negative thinking, negative relationship, or live in negative environment. These negative conditions sap oxygen and energy necessary to maintain balance from our physical body. Practice to become aware of, and stop engaging with, these negative thoughts.

2. Intention. Remain connected, regardless of your current situation, to your conscious and unconscious thoughts/feelings. Set your goal, daily, on baby step intention and remain consistent. This is key for any type of energetic movement. Even when you start to slip back to old pattern thinking, do your very best to remain strong and focus. Notice how you feel when you take a stand. Doubt is bound to creep in. Three to four days into this commitment can, and will, bring significant movement if you will maintain your diligent in knowing that there is light at the end of the tunnel, regardless of your current challenges.

3. Communicating Empowerment Phrases. Each day we have decisions and choices to make. From the time we wake up and decide to engage into our life, i.e. school, work, motherhood, marriage, we can choose to give it our best effort with thought and action, or we can remain in negative patterns which will cause us to react. Be mindful of our communication with ourself through our first thought which will set the stage for the entire day. If you truly want to bring change, joy, and personal comfort into your life, you must start with the positive thought and communication with yourself and others throughout the day.

4. Confirming Conclusion. Remind yourself: "My goal will be met through small, diligent baby steps." Keep the faith.

Reminder: You must be aware of the signs and symptoms of the *pattern* you want to change! You must have a strong desire to bring new energy to your life!

Write In Your Journal Daily For 30 Days

Feel yourself within and then answer the following questions. Take a minimum of 10 minutes to do this work. You are going to be identifying who you are and tracking patterns. You will be learning how to change your patterns as you create new ones.

Awareness is Key. Intention is Key. Most importantly, your core strength will approach this process with the awareness that you are not interested in living in the past that no longer serves you in a positive manner. Awareness is fundamental in creating the process of a new pattern. Awareness with repetition, as a tool to success, will allow this shift to take place.

Dig deep. Try to create sacred, quiet time to reunite with your inner core. Take this slowly and listen to the answers that present themselves from within your intuition and your body. If you feel any discomfort, like a tight stomach, stop, breathe, and then ask, *"What am I feeling?"* It is the clue that is leading you to yourself!

1. **The Questions:**
    - ☐ What are you all about?
    - ☐ What do you know about yourself?
    - ☐ What do you hide about yourself?
    - ☐ What do you expect from yourself?
    - ☐ What do you want in your daily life?
    - ☐ What do you want in the big picture of your life?
    - ☐ What do you want others to know about you?
    - ☐ What do you want to keep from others?

2. **The Commitment:** For the next 30 days, repeat this exercise to confirm your thoughts and your decisions. You can, and will, grow and change through the process. Allow yourself to identify more and more with your desires, hopes, and dreams. Choose large and small goals and visions. Do not judge your hopes and dreams against others. For one person, a hope may be to live another day. For another, it might be buying a new home or finding a career that is meaningful. Do not judge your hopes and dreams. Experience them through your self-assurance and your core desires.

3. **The Rules:** *Stop living or identifying with the past.* Make sure you identify what critical or negative thoughts come up as you write. Notice how you might find yourself living in the past.

You need to acknowledge these thoughts, write them down, then cross them out. This is an imperative step to gaining and re-establishing self-confidence and self-esteem. *You must stop living in the past.* Do not repeat the same story day-after-day. This goal can be easily accomplished if you are diligent in your commitment.

Remember: You are learning a new skill: how to remodel your thought processes. Every time a thought comes up from the past, write it down, cross it out, and say out loud *stop.* Then say: *This thinking cannot nor will not serve my new life, my new desires, or my new self.*

Just as you think the old thoughts that bring negativity, heartache, sadness, and angry feelings, you can begin to create the new feelings, desires, and hopes. You choose. It is truly that simple.

Enhance the Process with Empowerment Phrases

Repeat these empowerment phrases throughout your day. Choose at least 2 that feel right. Speak them out loud or whisper them. Look at yourself in the mirror as you speak or say them silently to yourself:

- ☐ I do not feel comfort or safety living in the past. I am free to move forward with the confidence and self-assurance I feel right now.

- ☐ My past no longer dictates my future. I live in peace with past decisions and choices.

- My feelings of despair, fear, and loss are in the past. When I am ready, I will move forward with self-assurance. When I am ready, my spirit will re-attach itself to my core self.

- I am able to support my life with the choices and decisions I make.

- I am able to put the past to rest. I am able to create new experiences each day, based upon what I know I deserve and am capable of.

- The thoughts I create based upon my hopes and dreams of the future far out-weigh the thoughts and feelings of the past.

- Allowing myself to feel the freedom of the future allows me to disconnect from the past.

You are the creator of your life. Regardless of when you start to wake up to that idea, *and own it*, you are in charge. Allow yourself to live in your life each day. Whatever may have happened in the past, it is gone. The pain can live on as long as you allow it to live. Suffering is painful. I know this on a very deep level of understanding. I also know that there are just two choices: staying here--a dead end street, replaying the same old story day in day out, or, moving forward--which can be painful, but you can take it as slow as you need to.

The experiences you have had are just that: an experience, or many experiences. Without wanting more for the future, the energy stagnation will remain the same. A strong desire is imperative for movement if you have had challenges in living *daily* in the past.

For many, the past is like a warm blanket that initially was filled with thorns, tears, discolor, and uncomfortableness. And after a while, somehow, it became the most comfortable piece of cloth imaginable. It is not easy to let go of the past as many might want us to believe. The past holds a lot of weight and power. When we choose to let go, believing the now and future have a better fit for us, we start to move and remove the stagnation. It is the beginning to rebuilding the future based upon what you hope to create. Do not be afraid. I have confidence that you have it within you what it takes to create the life you truly desire! Regardless of how long it may take you to accomplish it.

Chapter 4.

THE LOVE ENERGY CENTER

> Heart Energy
>
> I truly love myself and know that others feel I love them too.

Significance: Giving and accepting of one's personal interpretation of love. Creating relationships with openness. Not afraid of giving to others. Allowing free flow in relationships of affection and support. Feeling love without conditions and expectations. Giving and feeling compassion freely. Acceptance of one's true self. Feeling hope and understanding. Supporting others in your life. Words of encouragement to others that come freely and without thought. Feeling a connection to self. Feeling a comfort inside that is not easily swayed by experiences or moments.

Balanced: We feel our personal understanding of love, and feel securely connected to everything and everyone in our life. A feeling of giving without thought or expectation of outcome. Speaking from a place of affection and compassion. Affection through words, actions, and reactions when communicating. Creating balance with those around you through your gentle affection and kind consideration. A feeling of having enough support in your own life.

Unbalanced: We can feel isolated, unloved, and overlooked. We can have difficulty breathing in new life, the feeling of living in life. Anxiety, deep sorrow, and confusion about *why* a person wants us or cares for us. Pushing away those who truly care and want to lend support. Not feeling loved, accepted, respected, or wanted even though the truth may be very different from the feeling inside. Wanting love and affection without the tools to support the energy in life. Using sexual energy and clever words and actions to get what we want from others. Anxiety, cardio challenges, and excessive pain and stress of and near the shoulder blades can all be a challenge of the love energy.

ঌ∞ঌ∞ঌ∞ঌ∞ঌ∞ঌ

Love may be the most incredible energy available for humans to give and to receive. It can create ultimate pleasure and fulfillment, and yet, within minutes, it can destroy the essence of the soul. It can rip the very spirit of us to shreds within a moment. At times, for some of us, never to recover fully.

Why does love affect us so deeply? How can love tear our soul to shreds, never to recover? What is that mechanism within our mental self or emotional self that can be so deeply affected?

Love energy is a profound and mysterious force. It is housed in and around our bodies but finds its home in the Heart or Love Energy Center. What is love energy? Is it a feeling or a thought? How do we know what love is and what it means? From the moment we are born, from the moment our mother or the first human being touches us, we need to feel comfort, safety, and connection. We know this instinctively. We know we want warm, cozy touch, and cuddle. We want that energy of someone who is naturally and lovingly providing warmth and comfort. As infants, we are certainly not using the word 'love'. We have absolutely no expectation or concept of what the word means. But from the minute we come into this world, we instinctively know how to express need through crying or voice noises to ask for warmth, a diaper change, calmness, cuddling, food, or any form of comfort. This is a natural phenomenon. Interestingly enough also is the energy of the soul at birth--it too wants to cuddle and give affection from its own spirit, not just receive.

We need food and safety. We desire and crave human affection. If we are able to obtain these key essentials, we feel secure, stable, content, and sheltered. If we could just continue with these needs for comfort and security through adulthood, we would feel blessed and content. For many civilizations in the past, this was enough. And this set of needs and wants, when fulfilled, could allow us to feel comfort and contentment in our life. But we have grown and evolved, we want, even expect, much more. We want intimacy, deep connection, even romance, plus a sense of purpose and fulfillment. We want this kind of love as adults. We have labeled what it looks like, feels like, and what we are willing to *give* to get it. And in some cases, what we will withhold until we get it or come close to it.

How we define the word 'comfort' and express the feelings of *love* are personal and quite individual in nature. There are very few people in this world who will define the feelings or the meaning of love in exactly the same words. We all crave and search for love. But how differently each of us defines this huge energy is often the reason that so many relationships are out of balance. Because of the misunderstanding behind the word 'love,' relationships can be destroyed as quickly as they felt promise and possibility. Love can be confusing. It can be dangerous. It can be transformational. As the meaning of love can include all those "the Good, the Bad, and the Ugly," the word 'love' can make or break the human spirit. It is amazing that love inhabits this heart center and can fill it or leave it empty. Knowing what one believes or wants to believe about love and having that basic personal understanding helps fill the gap.

The Complexity of the Heart/Love Energy Center

In my opinion, 'love' is the most complicated and complex word in the dictionary. Do you know that in some cultures, the word 'love' is not included in the dictionary? How do we know what it really means unless we know what we as individuals feel and understand it to be? The biggest misconception I have found in working with the word 'love' is the relevance and misunderstanding that is associated with it. One person believes love means X and the person they partnered with has a whole different meaning Y he or she attributes to, for the same word. Relationships can, and do, end in sorrow, disaster, and complete shut down of the participants because the word 'love' does not have a shared meaning! It is heartbreaking for couples and children to experience the often devastating results of this misconception.

A few definitions of the word 'love' are:

- Strong affection for another arising from kinship, personal ties, and family.
- Affection based upon sexual feelings.
- Warm attachment, devotion, admiration.
- Beloved person/persons.
- Unselfish loyal and benevolent concern for the good of another.
- Brotherly concern for others.
- Person's adoration of God.

And the list goes on. But it barely touches the surface of the depths of this word. That is because *love* is truly an energy in itself. Again, what one person feels the word 'love' means to him or her can be quite the opposite of another. The word 'love' is one of the most confusing, misunderstood, overly used, and grossly manipulated word in the human language.

What do we all want to hear? What do we all want to feel? What do we all want to experience? *Love, Love, Love!*

Why do we become extremely elated and feel euphoric when we hear the phrase, "I love you"?

Why do we feel deep despair, depression, confusion, and disconnect from our core and from the world when the *expectation* of love does not work out for us?

What happens to the human self when love is not available in the manner we *believe* we must have it delivered?

What happens to a child when a parent has told them for years and years that they love them and then, one day, they leave? Never to return.

What happens to a partner when all of a sudden, one day, out of the blue, their significant other tells them that they are leaving, that the *love* is just not there anymore?

Definitions and meanings of words are crucial. They are energetic vibrations in and of themselves. If we don't agree on what 'love' is, we can connect with another and find a lack of unity or congruity in our affection, expressions of caring, hopes, and dreams. It is really true that many *love* relationships are often in imbalance and fail to move into the place of total unity because we simply don't agree on this enigmatic word.

Six Varieties of Love Energy

There are many varieties of love energy. Here are descriptions of six of the most popular meanings/concepts. As you read through the information, imagine how difficult it is for couples and those looking for love to sift through what the meaning is for themself and then try to match that with the sense and understanding of the other. It can be exhausting, even for those who feel they are *in love*. Taking a truthful inventory of *your needs* when engaging in love helps.

What each of us defines as the *comfort* of love will define what we gravitate towards in our lifetime. If you are not sure what the word 'love' means to your partner, children, family, or significant other in relationships, you could, and often do, move through your life with an illusion created within your own identity. You may never understand the other person's concept or feelings about love. You are then incongruous with this very important person in the most significant ways.

Our parent/s or caregiver/s provide us with our initial experience of the feeling and meaning of love. This word may or may not be heard nor experienced from an early age. Many of us have never heard the words: "I love you." Many hear the phrase: "I'll love you if you do …. or I'll love you if you are …." How love entered our lives defines how we feel about loving and being loved. To some, being loved can make them terribly uncomfortable. They might feel that they owe something, that there are strings with being loved. We either identify with it comfortably, or we do not. Even though we desperately and secretly desire love, we may never put ourselves in a position to truly experience love because of the mix messages the *love* experience has for us.

There are many ways we experience the feeling of love and our early experience of love is an imprint that will remain with us through a lifetime. We can add to it, subtract from it, but we will never forget our first introduction. We either experienced it from a compassionate, generous, and open heart or we experienced it from a place of non-attachment, expectation, conditions, and manipulation. We experienced it from a place of responsibility or a place of irresponsibility. How much or how little these experiences have been in our life and under what circumstances plays an important role in how we use the word 'love,' how we express our feelings associated with the word 'love,' and, most importantly, our *expectation* behind the word and feelings of 'love.'

The *expectation of love* will cripple all who attach their listed expectation to a heart-felt, compassionate relationship. It can be the death to the very soul of the individuals involved. Because no two families or two parent combinations operate or interpret love relationships the same way, it is very hard to imagine two people finding exact experiences to match their idea or feeling behind love.

Affection Love:

If the relationship with the parent/s or caregiver/s was that of affection and intimate or closeness, lots of touching and hugging, that child may attach the meaning of 'love' to that of affection, cuddling, hugging, holding hands, and perhaps even being kissed on the cheek or forehead. In this particular case, the child would certainly associate love with affection. If this pattern was consistent throughout this child's early childhood, this child would certainly grow up believing that affection is directly linked to love. He or she would want to show their affection by touching. If this child, as an adult, finds their way to a relationship he or she believes is *love worthy*, but their mate does not find 'affection' a part of their vocabulary of love, this person may end up with issues surrounding: self-assurance (stomach), love energy (chest), or passion energy (lower extremities). Not being able to express or receive the affection he/she has always known as the cornerstone to the relationship with love will be devastating.

Responsibility Love:

In a certain household, some parents are dutiful; the parent/s or caregiver/s are accountable and responsible. Perhaps there is a broken family and the father was the responsible parent during childhood. He may have gotten up very early in the morning, prepared the meals, assured the children of meeting the school day on time, and returning with them after his work day ended. For this parent, affection may not be as frequent and could be somewhat awkward, but the role and responsibility are one of great affection and comfort to him. Thus, feeling and believing that his child/children would understand the gesture-- that this was his way of showing his love and affection. If this behavior was consistent, he/she would have learned that having food consistently, having a roof over their head, obtaining an education, and having a few pairs of clean clothes was love--love that is not associated with the words or showing affection.

This child may not have the intimate experiences with physical affection or experiences of hearing a parent uses the phrase "I love you" or even use the word 'love.' But what they did experience was something very important to most, accountability. Being responsible for the choices you make in your life, which in this case is being a parent. Perhaps the parents showed their affection by always having food, always being home to help with homework, and always making sure that the clothing was clean. This child would certainly relate love to responsibility. If this was a consistent pattern, something that was constant over a long period of time throughout childhood, it is certain that this child would feel security with the responsibility feeling of love and affection.

If this child, as an adult, finds their way to a relationship he/she believes is *love worthy*, and the mate does not find 'accountability' or 'responsibility' a part of their vocabulary of love, this person may end up with an imbalance within the core self. For this adult, he/she may find a challenge with a mate who does not accept responsibility in areas that are core issues within a family unit or a serious committed relationship. In that case or something similar they may experience challenges with stability (lower extremities) and communication (throat) energy. Not having a partner displaying responsible traits and values will be a challenge.

Mixed Message Love:

In another household, we may have a family with a parent/s or caregiver/s who experience issues with alcohol, anger, drug addiction, or self-absorption. One parent may be the buffer between the parents with the above challenges and the child, or both parents may be experiencing one or more of these challenges simultaneously. If a parent or parents have personal challenges that involve this type of behavior, this child will have inconsistent feelings about the word 'love.'

Most addictive personalities have difficulty maintaining a sense of their own self. It would be fair to say that the children or a child of this type of parent/s may have uncertainty behind what love and comfort means. If there is anger in this house, abuse, or inability to maintain certain standards in this house, the child may not feel the necessary emotions consistently enough to understand what love, affection, and comfort is. This particular child may grow up with a feeling of distance and disconnect. Maintaining consistency will be a challenge in this person's journey.

As an adult, this person may have challenges in defining what stability is. When we have issues with stability, *love* is clearly a concept that is not easily understood. If the parent/s gave the vibration that *love* was attached to them not being abused, this child will think that very little, or none, in return in their relationships is acceptable. If the child felt *love* was not being yelled at more than two times a week, this child will understand that a compromised relationship that is somewhat painful is acceptable, just because it is not as painful and uncomfortable as their childhood experience. This adult may not expect much from life or the experience of love, or from relationship possibilities. If the child does not learn from a mentor or someone who truly loves them along the way, they may not reach their full potential in life. One of the many challenges this child/adult might have is: stability (lower extremities), communication (throat), self-assurance (stomach), and love (chest) energy. The possible combination of anxiety, fear, digestion, asthma, and the clear and concise flow of thought to verbal communication can be quite damaging. These four energy centers are essential for having energy, air, and nutrients flow through the body properly.

Performance Love:

If a child is born into a household that is based upon obligation or the need to achieve, they will associate the word 'love' to that of performance and excellence. They feel that they have to earn love through being the best. Needing to perform wears down a child's nervous system as well. The nervous system is needed to provide stability and comfort to the entire human system. Many children who have this type of energy around them suffer from anxiety, fear, and depression. They may also develop asthma.

Performance love is almost always about the presenter. We can trace it back to perhaps their parents or their caregivers, but, deep down, the challenges lies within their own self-confidence energy. Transferring this type of energy to a child creates restrictions. At times their world can become so small that they fear the very breath they need to actually live.

As an adult, if this person is not allowed to succeed, perform, or achieve, it can have lasting effects on the love energy (heart), self-assurance energy (stomach), wisdom energy (head), passion energy (male and female sexuality), and finally stability energy (lower extremities). If you are measured by success from a young age, the pressure of life can at times become unbearable. If you are paired at any time with a partner who is overly critical or governed by Mixed Message Love or Responsibility Love, you could see physical issues show up on a regular basis. This combination is a person who lives with high anxiety, extreme fear, very little sleep, and a disconnection to any type of comfort.

Physical Love:

If a child was brought up in an environment that revolves around their physical beauty, their ability to *look* a certain way or dress a certain way, or represent themself in a way that is acceptable in the outer world, this child will equate love to physical presence. If this is a female child, the child will look for exterior beauty in relationships and will also use their exterior beauty to find love in the world. If there was a child in this household who was not as attractive as expected or as those in the household, this child/young adult can have serious challenges with their identity, such as not feeling good enough and not feeling beautiful. This emotional scenario can manifest as ongoing energetic issues for a lifetime. The challenges can be seen in: love energy (heart), self-assurance energy (stomach), and passion energy (male and female organs, hormones).

Persona Love:

If you were born into a family of elite success on some level, the type of challenges you will interacting in creating a balance or understanding of *love* can be much more complex. When you are able to obtain material objects and use this material gain to interact in a life most will never understand or walk into, you have individual challenges that most people will never understand nor comprehend. I work with a client who has never written a check nor has ever been inside a bank. Never paid her own bills and has no concept whatsoever of what it costs to live in this world or her world. A set of challenges most of us will never need to concern ourselves with. That can certainly be a blessing!

Or, if you are the adult who lives with or has had elite success and you find that those you are attracting cause frustration because they don't seem to *know* the *real* you, this can cause obstruction in the flow of the energy of who you really are. So you sit wondering if the relationship is engaged with the real you or the "persona" you the public knows.

When you are introduced to a successful individual, you are immediately aware of their personal energy. They bring it with them everywhere they go. "This is …. (so and so)." A persona-- an energy in a class all of its own. You can become intrigued, fall in love with, become infatuated with, and become so overwhelmed with their energy, that you lose the very insight needed to discern *what* you love. This is difficult for both parties. The *persona* person wants to be loved for their true self, which is so tightly entwined with the persona self. The person loving or wanting to love this person can, and almost always do, fall in love with the persona and cannot quite overcome the reality that they are, at the bottom of it all, just a person, a human being. Many times, they give up their very essence for the opportunity to be with this persona person. Even if you are as famous as the person you are engaged with, each will have their own set of energetic challenges of acceptance. Both parties can have challenges with: self-assurance (stomach), communication (throat), wisdom (upper head), stability (lower extremities), and love (heart).

Love Is a Complex Subject

Love is a complex subject for most. For those who use the word often and lightly, it is not such a challenge. They use it, at times abuse it, and then have little to no guilt or responsibility when the feeling they once had, and reported to another, simply evaporated or was just no longer available or viable.

I have sat with couples and individuals discussing the challenges they feel surrounding having and lacking love. I can honestly say that it has caused the most confusion and the greatest sadness for those who suddenly, almost always too late, discovered that what they felt love meant wasn't exactly the truth for them and those they loved. They discover this after the love is gone, and the moment to recreate it is gone as well. They realize that their expectations were so out of line, so unreal, so self-centered, that it dissipated all the love and devotion that was once there. This realization can be devastating.

The Mind Over-Riding the Energy of Love

What happens when we express the word 'love'? Why do women want to use that word immediately in a relationship? Why do men want to run away from that word? What is it about the first person in a relationship who feels the feelings associated with love and requires that their partner says the words "I love you" so quickly? Why do men run away from having to say those words out loud? Why do men want to avoid hearing those words and feel extremely stressed when a woman says or implies them?

Why are so many books written on *how to* secure a partner? How to love your partner? How to know your partner's signals? How to understand men or women? The mystery is simple. The majority of people feel that finding someone to love is about strategy, wisdom, and cleverness. It is about *catching the prey*.

They feel that there is a technique. They feel that there is a payoff.

Even many so-called "love experts" suggest that if you follow the correct procedures and rules, you will find Mr. or Miss Perfect. I feel that unless you understand yourself and the meaning/expectation of what love and commitment mean to you, you are at a loss. In addition, you must have an understanding of a potential partner's personal meaning of love and know their expectations in a relationship. Without this basic understanding, there is little possibility of long, lasting, fulfilling love.

Love is an equation that is colored differently for everyone. Understanding your personal meaning of love is the number one rule to understanding and loving yourself. To build a firm and energetically sound love platform, you need to establish your own deep connection to what 'love' means to you.

You also need to know what you expect in return for what you give, that is, what you really *need* in relation to expressing your version of love. Until this set of expectations and meanings are defined and aligned within, expressing, receiving, and interacting in the essence of love can be complicated, confusing, and may even cause great strain and emotional stress and trauma. That is why, for the fragile and meek, the breakup of a loving relationship can be devastating. Regardless of the inner structure of what that relationship is, we are attracted to certain individuals for many reasons. They help us understand ourselves. Know what you want in your life. Know what feels right for you. Do not compromise your inner self, your soul self, your little light within. Don't you dare strip away the beauty of who you are and what you desire in a relationship. Someone is out there to engage with you in a healthy, heartfelt, and loving manner. Believe it!

Two Different Loves: the Athlete and the Model Story

Cleve was an incredibly successful athlete. In his early thirties, he was set and solid in his career. His father taught him to get his life in order before he became engaged in a long term relationship and Cleve waited until he felt ready and available. Cynthia was a young forceful woman who came from flighty, unstable, divorced parents. Cleve was the son of very stern, responsible, and fully committed parents. Cynthia had difficulty in school and had a great need to prove herself in the world. Despite their essential differences, Cleve loved Cynthia and Cynthia felt huge possibilities with Cleve.

A year into the relationship, Cleve asked Cynthia to marry him. Cynthia did not know that Cleve was that interested in her. She was in disbelief and full of excitement. How could she, a girl from a broken home who was always on the move with her mother and without a real sense of place, attract such a successful and decent man? Was it all the confidence she exuded from winning so many beauty contests when she grew up? Was it her charm? She questioned her relationship from the beginning. Why me?

A huge 3 carat diamond ring was placed on her finger. Cleve was secure with his decision and he knew that he could provide for his wife and future family. He was confident that his career would take him successfully into his 37th year and he knew that he was set for the future. The wedding was everything Cynthia could have dreamed of. Cleve spared no expense to give his new bride all that she wanted. He had a great time seeing her excitement as she prepared for the big day.

Cleve sat down with Cynthia to go over the conditions of the marriage. His father suggested he talk to Cynthia about his role as father, husband, and provider. He modeled his words after the serious talk he had with his dad some years earlier. He needed her to understand that his work took him away several months every year and that for the next 7 years, he would be away quite often. She didn't seem to mind. Cleve and Cynthia were already planning to hire the assistance Cynthia needed to maintain their home. She was very hopeful and felt great pride in Cleve's status as an elite athlete. Cleve was content. He had crossed all the t's and dotted all the i's. Cynthia was floating on cloud nine, still intoxicated by her remarkable custom designer wedding dress and beautiful big ring!

When it was time to purchase a home, Cynthia started to change her attitude toward Cleve's wealth. In the beginning, she was nervous about spending too much, did not want to over-indulge, and did not want to over-reach. Cleve was very impressed with his new wife's approach to finances and her lack of need to be with the "in crowd." But, because of his status, she was spun into the celebrity life very quickly. This life did not affect Cleve. He had signed his first contract at the age of 21. He was well into his ninth year of great, well-earned success. He was not interested in drugs or excessive alcohol. He enjoyed his career and wanted to settle down to the life of a married man, hoping to have a few children along the way.

The house the couple eventually purchased was well over the 2 million-dollar budget Cleve set. It caused a bit of discomfort since Cleve was a planner, but he wanted to make his new wife happy. Cynthia was elated. She was basking in the glory of her new found upscale life. When she started to choose the furnishings for her beautiful home, she learned from a new girlfriend that a *decorator* was the right way to professionally decorate the home. That people of this stature do not do-it-yourself home decorating. So, she hired a decorator, which cost nearly $150K, without consulting Cleve. Cynthia rationalized the expense by stating that she did not have enough experience to purchase furniture for such a huge home. Cleve was not happy. He wanted his wife to participate with him in purchasing and selecting the furniture. This was the first of many unsettling conversations between the two.

They enjoyed the first 3 months of marriage without much conflict. It was apparent to Cleve that Cynthia's closet was increasingly being stuffed with new items. Without discussing with Cleve, Cynthia began spending large sums of money. Cleve sat down with Cynthia to communicate, in a matter of fact manner, his concern with the increase of Cynthia's unnecessary purchases. This created a very unsettling feeling within Cynthia. She started to cry and demanded to know if Cleve *really loved* her.

Cleve did not know how to answer that question nor did he understand why that question came up surrounding her over-spending. He calmed her down with his gentle words. He explained to Cynthia that over-spending was not a good pattern. He wanted her to fill her days with other activities. He was concerned that she'd become like his friends' wives and become a huge consumer without any other real interests. He cautioned her to maintain the sense of herself she had prior to their marriage. Cynthia tried to listen but didn't hear the depth of what Cleve was saying. He wanted to warn her to avoid the traps of the entitled life but she was unable to realize that. She withdrew from hearing the words that could have saved her marriage.

It was time for Cleve to set out on his traveling schedule. He would be on the road, on and off, for several weeks, and eventually, several months. Cynthia did not feel pressure as she had new friends who were occupying her time. Cleve would call home to find that Cynthia was rarely ever there. She was out with her friends, dancing and drinking at all the *hot* spots. He found out through his friends' wives just how often Cynthia was out on the town. He did not like hearing the news. He called Cynthia often asking her to find other activities. She could not hear Cleve. Her credit cards were maxed out, after charging thousands of dollars on couture clothing and upscale jewelry and handbags.

What had happened to his wife? Who was she becoming? Or, who was she all along?

When Cleve arrived back home from a long working trip, Cynthia was not home to greet him. She was with her friends. She did not feel that it was necessary to reunite with Cleve the moment he walked through the door. When she finally came home later that night, Cleve asked her why she did not feel that it was important to be there when he returned. She simply said she was busy. This was very upsetting for Cleve. He was at the end of his rope. He did not yell or use abusive language. He went to bed. Cynthia did not try to comfort him.

The following morning Cleve sat down with Cynthia to talk about their relationship. She really didn't know what to say. She did not feel that her behavior was an issue while Cleve felt it was: over-spending, out all night, not answering phone calls, or not greeting him when he returned home after a time away. These were huge problems for Cleve.

Cynthia's response was simple, "What do you want from me?" He did not know how to reply. He did not expect this response. He did not realize just how serious the discord between his reality and her reality really was. It was at that very moment that Cleve realized that Cynthia did not understand how a male and female related to each other in marriage. Or, that a committed loving relationship is based upon core values. At that moment, his intuition kicked in. He knew there was trouble ahead. He wanted to help Cynthia understand how wonderful their life together could be, but knew deep inside it might not be a journey that they will take together. He made plans to take her out of town for the few days he had before the next trip.

They had a wonderful time outwardly, but inwardly Cleve felt that she was different. When they were together intimately, it was not the slow, long, passionate process as it was in the beginning during the planning of the marriage or the first few months afterwards. Cynthia wanted him to *hurry up* and *get it over*. It was not a pleasurable experience for her. Cleve clearly felt that it was work for her. He wanted to experience that beautiful woman he married, that tender touch, that compassionate kiss, that excitement that was electric between them in the beginning. Unfortunately, it was not to be.

After returning home, Cynthia jumped back into the relationships with her party friends. She was content. Cleve was lonely, depressed, and feeling unloved. Cleve left again on a traveling work trip. He was gone for several months. A friend of him heard from his wife that Cynthia was having an affair with a celebrity she met at a famous club in Los Angeles. Cleve could not believe it. He did not want to believe it. He did not want to think about it or react to it. He needed to focus on his work. The calls to Cynthia were less and less until, finally, he just stopped calling. He was hoping deep down that she would start to initiate the phone calls as she had in the beginning. Also, he remembered the time when she confessed her *love*, the affection he felt when they were intimate, and the overall feeling of hope and happiness they spoke of when they planned their marriage.

When Cleve returned home, his wife was again not there to greet him. He sat patiently until she walked through the door. Drunk and unpredictable, she sat down to discuss a topic that Cleve needed answers to. Was she having an affair? Was she still *in love* with him? Cynthia had just enough alcohol to blurt it out: "Yes, I was sleeping with another man; yes, I am still in love with you; and yes, I still want to remain in this marriage." Cleve was shocked. He sat in fear, anger, and complete confusion. He did not understand what his wife was saying. He heard the words but did not understand the meaning behind them. He left the room silently. He slept in a spare bedroom that night.

When he awoke, he sat in bed trying to gather his thoughts. He needed to discuss the marriage, the relationship, and her ideas of what was happening between the two of them. Cynthia was very clear when she started to speak. She told Cleve that she did love him. That she felt grateful that he wanted her as his wife, but, that she was not comfortable being with just one man. She felt that her *looks* were a huge part of who she was. She wanted to use her looks to obtain as much happiness as possible. Her idea of 'happiness' was the affection and attention she received from men. Particularly men who wanted her sexually.

He sat in disbelief. She tore out his heart with her words that had absolutely no feeling or emotion attached to them. Her words were very "matter of fact." What he learned at that very moment was tearing his heart and self-esteem apart. He sat in his chair crying. Cynthia did not express too much emotion. She asked if Cleve wanted a divorce. He sat staring at her for what seemed to be eternity. "Yes," he said softly, "I would like a divorce."

Her next question was without any emotion: "Can you tell me how much money I can take with me?" He said, "Enough to live on."

When Cleve came to my office wanting help to resolve the chest pain, stomach challenges, and heart ache, I did not want to believe his story. I needed to really hear it from Cynthia. There were parts of what Cleve lived through that he needed to reconfirm. The devastation was unreal for him. She agreed to a lengthy recap of her time with Cleve. My thoughts and feelings were with both Cleve and Cynthia. The story was such a tragedy. By phone, she confirmed the entire story. Even though I knew it was true, I did not want it to be true. Not for Cynthia, not for Cleve. Cynthia will remain, throughout her lifetime, searching for love, *real* love. She brought Cleve into her life to show her and experience with her the *true meaning* of love. Unfortunately, she did not know what it looked like or felt like.

Cleve had the affection, the stability, and was capable of creating the comfort effortlessly. Because of Cynthia's loneliness and empty childhood experiences, she was not able to *embrace* that. She was still in the mode of going from relationship to relationship, trying to find the stability and love she craved as a child. Although she had created what her heart truly desired, and could have stayed in a stable, loving lifestyle forever with the man who loved her dearly, she did not recognize and was not able to enjoy the energy of stable and loving family. She had never experienced it and so could not appreciate it. She could not get out of her, though painful yet familiar, past childhood experience--it is here for a moment and then she must move on to the next opportunity.

Because of Cleve's upbringing, he believed that everyone wanted the life he and his family had growing up. He thought a woman would be proud and fulfilled to have such a man with his respectful, stable, and loving (from his perception). What he did not understand, and was not aware of, is that not everyone feels love in the same way. Cleve learned through the toughest and most painful experience, that 'love' means something completely different to each person who speaks the word.

A year later, I caught up with Cleve. He was still single, traveling with his work, and slowly recovering from the devastating experience. Cynthia, sadly, spent her settlement. She did not buy a home, did not invest, and no longer had her "friends" in Los Angeles.

Creating Love & Healing

RECONNECTING WITH YOUR LOVE ENERGY CENTER

Have you ever wondered what is stored in your heart area? What you are truly feeling about love, your life, and the healing that may need to occur? This is not an exercise to open up the heart of those around you. Its purpose is one of self-discovery and self-love. Understanding your connection to love, the meaning and feeling, not only will you define and refine what love means to you, but you will also learn to align with and accept your personal interpretation.

Make yourself as comfortable as you are able. Prepare a space for yourself to be alone, perhaps some music, light a candle, and prepare to engage in a true "heart to heart" connection with yourself. Make sure you have a pen and paper nearby. Sense how you feel inside. Focus your attention on your stomach, heart, and lungs. Now breathe as deeply as you are able, slowly, no hurry, no rush. Breathe in and out again, slowly. One more time. Three is about communication.

After you have relaxed with your breath, please tap slowly and gently on your chest area. Very gently, knock on the heart center to access the love and healing energy of the heart. Please do this three times, gently and slowly. You are gently tapping on the heart area in preparation of this energy center's participation with you. The intention you have, the breathing, and tapping is now preparing this energy center to work with you in creating understanding and balance.

Sit back, relax, and simply acknowledge your heart. The essence of what your true feelings are. When you access this area of your body, emotional release can occur. Allow for a moment to understand any emotion you will experience. No one will experience the same moment. Know that your moment in connecting with your heart, your love, and healing energy is personal.

The questions I feel can create a secure bond between the emotional energy, mental energy, spiritual energy, and physical energy are:

- What does my heart feel today? Right now, what does my heart feel and what do I need to acknowledge that is top on the list?

- How does my heart affect the way I interact with others?

- If I could express my feelings to a person in my life who I want to communicate with, what would I say?

- How do people interpret me in my life today?

- What do I want to express about myself to others that is difficult?

- What do I want to say to my spouse/lover who creates conflict within me?
- What do I want to say to my children to let them know how much I love them?
- What do I need to do to create a loving relationship with myself?
- What are the qualities about myself that are loving?
- How can I create a consistent pattern of living with compassion?
- What do I really want in my life that I am lacking? That is connected to my heart?
- Who do I want to express my feelings to that is difficult for me?
- What do I need to leave in the past that cannot move with me into the future?
- Who needs more love from me?
- Who needs to feel my true feelings about them?
- Who do I want to express my inner truth to?
- If I could say one thing to the person I love deeply, what would that be?

How do you use this information? Start applying it today. The answers that you have just heard and are now exploring are of importance. The energy that is attached to love, being loved, sharing love, and accepting love is one of the most important connections we have. It is the one that, for most, we cannot truly live without. The energy of the heart is awake within us all. I know we do not feel it as often as we should or could. The pressures of life, the past, the disappointments, and the confusion cloud and create a barrier. Please do not give up! Make this energy center a priority for you each and every day until you feel the balance and understanding that feels most comfortable for you. If you have ever had challenges or soreness in the shoulder blade area, this can be confirmation that you are holding onto past pain in the heart area. This is a holding area, a shield if you will. As you start to release this stagnant energy by using your words, truth, and strength of energy movement, you will find that connecting to what you want in your emotional self will become much easier and with less restriction. Speaking the words--communicating the truth to yourself--is the start of loosening this energy so the feelings flow easily and with little to no effort. The heart area must have space to accept the free flow of emotional energy associated with expression of love to flow freely. Removing the stagnation is the first step.

Chapter 5.

The Communication Energy Center

Communication Energy

My words express my integrity, truth, and my inner feelings.

Significance: Smoothness in communicating one's thoughts and feelings. Ability to speak openly without restriction, distress, emotional upset, or angry outbursts. Our center of expression to the world and those in our lives. The energy behind our thoughts and emotions. A base point to communicate our affection, love, and sexual needs to others. Our ability to say what we want to others without feelings of humiliation or estranged.

Balanced: We feel and release, from our voice, free flowing words and expression of oneself. Ability to communicate to those surrounding us with clarity, feeling, and compassion. Feeling secure with the intention of our thoughts and words that we express to ourselves and others. Not feeling a need to hide our feelings from others.

Unbalanced: We feel we must censor our words and expressions to be accepted. We may speak without conviction and speak too quickly or too softly. We may express ourselves from a place of fear and anxiety, resulted from forceful pent-up emotional expression. We may not have the confidence to express our inner most feelings resulting in never or rarely being heard, accepted, or known for our true self. Holding feelings in that associated with our desires, needs, and wants from those around us. Stagnation and areas of concern in the thyroid, throat, ears, and collar bone area can be a challenge of the communication energy.

☙☙☙☙☙

What is communication energy? It is the energy associated with our thoughts. This very powerful center communicates what percolates inside of our hearts and minds out through our vocal chords into the world. Every thought we have is translated into *mental chatter*, inner dialogue, and other forms of non-verbal communication or verbal communication. How important is this energy center in the connection to creating and experiencing abundance, joy, love, and pleasure? Extremely important!

This energy center will work for or against us in obtaining what we want in life. If we cannot communicate to others what we feel inside--the very essence of what we want, need, and know--we can, and do, become stuck. This energy center can actually suck the wind from our sails. If blocked, we may feel suffocated or smothered. We may experience difficulty breathing, swallowing, or speaking. When the energy of our thoughts and feelings get *stuffed*, it almost always moves from the Communication Energy Center in our throat down into our chest. When this occurs, it often manifests as anxiety, panic, or distress. The heart center is just below this energy center. If it is emotional energy that needs to be released but is blocked, it shoots right back down into the Love Energy Center or heart area.

When the words we need to communicate are, for any reason, rejected by our inner critic, what we *need to* or *must* say remains in limbo. Now, this thought or feeling does not leave our consciousness. It does not disappear; instead, it hovers "somewhere," waiting for just the right moment to be released, to be communicated. And, it will not be always expressed when we want to express it! This is evident in challenging confrontations inside of core relationships between employees and bosses, parents and children, couples, and close friends. Have you ever heard a grown adult confessed the distress and anger they felt because of their *argument* with a two or three years old kid? What could a two to three years old child possibly communicate that could bring up the *feelings* of an adult transforming that conversation into a fight? Exactly my point. When this communication center becomes inflamed, volatile, constricted, and overwhelmed, the voice of reason and words can quickly become distorted. Rarely, if ever, is the moment of release about the topic at hand.

How many times have you truly needed to communicate something that was difficult to express? How many times have you wished you had said something but did not or could not? Think back to a specific situation. Do you remember what it felt like to have stifled your strong feelings and thoughts? Did you feel nervous, afraid, or possibly suddenly exhausted? Some people can actually lose sleep over this kind of repression. Others find themselves tongue-tied and reach for another glass of wine.

The energy behind our thoughts and feelings connects us to our true self, our inner soul or spirit. When we shut down our Communication Energy Center and diminish the value of our feelings and thoughts, we reduce our self-esteem and sense of self-worth. For many, this can lead to severe anxiety and the feeling that we cannot breathe fresh air into our bodies for nourishment and relief. It can lead to a disconnection from those we love as well as shutting down to experiences we desire to participate in.

I have worked with literally thousands of individuals who did not understand the profound link between what they said to themselves (their inner dialogue or self-talk) and the actual tangible effect of these seemingly silent words on their outer world or environment. Our thoughts create our reality. Our thoughts, spoken or unspoken, have a direct impact on how we live or experience our lives.

Stifling Our Communication Energy Center

How is communication energy associated with life? How is it associated with the mind, body, or spirit of a person? How important is the simple act of speaking our truth? How important is it to say what's on our mind and in our heart? It is imperative! It is the core of how we introduce and express our inner feelings. Then, why are most of us unable to communicate from a place of confidence, ease, and integrity? Why have we lost the power of expression? Here are eight common responses people have shared:

- Fear of rejection.
- Fear of being judged.
- Fear of not being accepted.
- Fear of speaking from a place less intelligent than others.
- Fear of reprimand. losing position in life, career, or relationship/s.
- Fear of being misunderstood.
- Fear of not being loved.

Does any of these ring a bell? Fear is the common thread that ties together these eight reasons to shut down and not speak our truth. Fear runs the show, and eventually it runs our creativity, love, and health into the ground.

I am going to go out on a limb to suggest that many of us do not even speak our truth to that one very special person in our lives. It could be a best friend, a lover, our spouse, or a person we just met who holds a promise of a great relationship. As you read these words, think hard. Are there secrets, inner thoughts, or feelings that are important to you that you have not been able to express or communicate? This is the other important area when we look at the communication energy.

It is not just about expressing our truth in our daily life; it is about the huge issues that we keep inside, almost locked down within ourselves. This communication energy runs deep; it holds the thoughts and feelings about past experiences that are charged with tons of energy and, often, judgment. The energy behind these types of feelings is of the utmost importance to us. If we cannot share these thoughts and feelings with anyone, we must learn to share them with ourself. Is it important to tell everything about ourselves to others? Absolutely not. It is only important to communicate our feelings and thoughts of truth to ourself.

Having No Voice

The communication energy can become stagnant from an early age. Many children have had the unfortunate experience of not being heard in their youth. It is painful to have never had a voice within a family structure. Although many people grow up *seemingly* well-adjusted, some will never find their true voice. Some will rely on others to create relationships that do not allow them to utilize their brilliance or ideas, or to live their hopes and dreams. This pattern is sadly often a pattern for life. These people falsely believe "less is more." The less they communicate, the less they face rejection, loss of love, humiliation, and conflict, and the less they will have to suffer. But their beliefs create fear and constriction that then contracting their world until it shrinks.

And, they shrink with it. They mean well, but end up reducing themselves to accept whatever necessary to remain hidden from their soul's desire to participate through their own thoughts and feelings.

How many people do you know, individually or in relationships, who *bite their tongue* or *sedate* themselves in order to live in situations and operate in environments that are obviously detrimental to their mental, physical, and emotional health? How many people do you know who have learned to suffer through a life that is obviously repressive and unhealthy?

Somewhere along the line in their life, they learned the pattern of compromise. They shut down their Communication Energy Center. Where do their feelings go? What do you think happens when we stuff the feelings inside ourselves year-after-year-after-year? What happens in relationships with our employers who will not allow us to speak up? What happens when we shut down and do not share our opinions as staff members or executives? What happens to the husband or wife who is no longer being heard by their partner? What happens to a child who cannot seem to get anyone to listen to their little voice?

The Communication Energy Center is the key to being heard and seen or not being heard or seen. Our ability to speak when necessary, being heard by others, or being understood through our words all are imperative to living in our life so that we feel important, valued, and substantial!

Communicating what we truly want to say is freedom!

Our feelings and thoughts are who we are!

Express yourself!

If we are not expressing our inner thoughts, wisdom, and feelings, we are not being understood or truly known by those in our life. When we restrict the thoughts and feelings we are compelled to speak, we can cause a great deal of physical and spiritual imbalance. If we are unable to express ourselves with honesty and with an easy flow, we are suppressing the very essence of who we are.

Begin to Speak and Reconnect

At what point in life do we lose our voice? At what point do we finally say to ourself: "The struggle is just not worth it"? At what point do we know that we have passed the point of no return--that we have somehow disappeared into non-existence?

Have you ever noticed that in the clutter and noise of today's society, we rarely have a moment to even say hello to someone we care about? This can also be a sign that we are over-burdened within our own self. Communication is a viable and resourceful manner of energy recharge! What does it feel like when we talk to someone whom we love speaking to? Instant recharge! What does it feel like when we stop to take 5 minutes to call a loved one who is on our mind? Why do we not allow ourselves the time to really connect and check in?

If you or anyone you know is having trouble communicating, take a moment to speak to them. Start to reconnect. Begin the dialogue with someone you love or care for. Gently speak to them from a compassionate place. We all know of those who have shut down. It takes very little effort to engage a conversation with a fellow human being. I am not suggesting that we all become psychotherapists; I am merely suggesting a gentle 'I care about you' approach. Communication is the essence of our self-expression. It is the conduit for our thoughts and feelings! Use this energy wisely. Choose words and thoughts that are positive, meaningful, and filled with optimism.

Negative thoughts can, and will, work against you. From the moment you think the thought to the moment you express that feeling verbally to those around you, you are holding onto a form of personal poison. Be cautious. Become aware, on a daily basis, that your thought, negative or positive, holds energy. Awareness is the key to evaporating negative thoughts and patterns of thinking. Awareness is the key to communicating your thoughts and feelings, manifesting the abundance, love, pleasure, and accomplishment you desire and deserve.

Alice's Story

In 1994, I worked with a woman named Alice. Sadly, as you'll discover as you read on, Alice's husband's vulnerability to her continuous challenges resulting in his own physical health issue, ultimately resulting in his inability to breathe in life. For years, Alice had symptoms including insomnia, stomach indigestion, headaches, and anxiety, to name a few. They were not understood or successfully treated by her regular physicians. No one could help her. After much expense, she began to search for answers outside the box. Alice and I agreed to work on her energetic imbalances over a four week program to identify the patterns that created the greatest dysfunction in her daily life. She told me her story and over time we began to put together the pieces.

Alice began to see that the life she had been living over the past 9 years had created a sense of unhappiness. A few years into her marriage, she noticed that she lacked the drive to cook, clean, and engage in sexual relations with her husband. She loved doing those things before her marriage. At the beginning of her change of heart, James, her husband, did not mind. He remembered her fun loving and carefree spirit. He figured it was just a phase. As time went by, James realized that he did not have a voice in the relationship and gradually allowed her to disconnect from him and her commitment to their partnership. Since she had always been the driving force in the relationship, he seemed to have no choice other than accepted and submitted to her withdrawal, with much sadness. He also told me that, from an early age, he was taught that his voice and feelings did not matter. He was used to playing second fiddle.

Originally, James had signed up to be with the woman he adored and enjoyed. Together, they planned many adventures for their future. Alice in turn signed up to be cared for, just as her mother had. However, James seemed to feel that there would be a more equal give and take in the relationship. Obviously, they had two very different ideas and intentions going into the marriage, which they never really discussed or acknowledged. Although James agreed to financially care for Alice, he did expect them to work as a team. He wanted Alice to participate in his life. He wanted them to engage in the same activities as pre marriage. He wanted her to embrace hobbies, friendships, and organizations that were close to his own convictions. Alice quickly became disconnected. She was not able to interact with any type of enthusiasm or joy. She started to feel used and incomplete. The distortion she felt about her life took on a life of its own.

As Alice and I worked together each week to create a new sense of awareness and empowerment within her, the energy of the relationship started to shift. She began to *see* her husband as a benefit instead of someone to ignore. She even began to cook meals when he returned from work. Through new found awareness, Alice began to feel love again. She also felt stronger and more at home in her body.

After the weeks were up and the program had come to a conclusion, Alice went off on her own to create a more intimate relationship with her husband. She found that cooking meals for him, cleaning his clothing, and waking up in the morning to greet him with affection all made her happier and more in balance and at peace.

A few months later, I received a phone call from Alice that James was sick. During the years, she went from doctor to doctor, clinic to clinic, and she had not paid any attention to his health. He was always the provider. How could he be sick? He never got sick nor took time from work because of illness. Throughout the years, she never asked or knew if there were funds for her hospital hopping or her numerous outlets for healing possibilities.

Upon the news of his illness, Alice suddenly became concerned with finances. Finances were never a concern while she spent thousands of dollars on "short fix" cures with no long term effect. During a routine examination for his health insurance, the radiologist found a large tumor in her husband's chest. The biopsy came back as stage 4 lung cancer. Through further diagnostic testing, they also found tumors in his throat area (the Communication Energy Center). The physicians urged him to check into the hospital immediately for treatment.

Alice had told me that James often felt as though he could not breathe. But, because she was so busy with her own misery, Alice was not able to hear her husband's respond. He was in the middle of a toxic and stale home environment and could not breathe. He was stifled and shut down. He tried over and over again to help Alice instead of himself. Neither Alice nor her husband listened to his needs. Within four months, he passed away.

The lungs, according to what I am able to see energetically, are directly linked to the ability to breathe into life. For so many years, Alice had drained her husband with her reoccurring challenges, with no remedies or conclusion. The energy, finances, and lack of affection for years ultimately drained him of his life force. When we are unable to communicate our truth to others, especially those we love, stagnation and inflammation can create serious complications. For years, Alice's husband was in pain over the relationship but had not developed the communication skills nor the confidence (because of his childhood issues) to speak to Alice openly and honestly. He simply went on until he could no longer function.

Creating Free Flowing Words & Thoughts

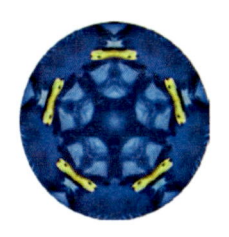

RECONNECTING WITH YOUR COMMUNICATION ENERGY

Many health issues can arise from the inability to speak the truth. So many of us have been shut down through various harsh experiences, criticisms, and conflicts. It is time to speak our truth. This verbal exercise needs to be practiced on a regular basis. Over time, you will be amazed at how you build self-confidence and a new voice that speaks with strength, self-love, and compassion.

This is a very simple technique. Here is how you can implement this process:

- Sit or stand in front of a mirror.
- Look yourself right in the eye(s) and smile. Feel yourself, feel your energy.
- Now, talk to yourself. Tell yourself all about whatever is weighing heavy on your heart and mind! Whatever it is, whatever is important to you, just say it.

- ☐ Communicate it out loud. Allow the energy attached to this important information to flow from your lips into the air. It may at first come out like a whisper. Or it might sound insincere or flat.

- ☐ Continue for at least 5 minutes, no matter how this process makes you feel. Refrain from judgment.

- ☐ Trust that you are doing something profound that will improve your health and your ability to feel in balance and in your own power, inside and out in the world.

After a few weeks of empowering yourself with your own truth on a daily basis, you may be ready for human communication. Let's see!

The first step in speaking your truth to someone whom you have created a sense of *lack of confidence* within yourself in the past can proceed like this:

- ☐ Feel within your core self what you would like to say.

- ☐ Comfortably communicate the words you would like to say.

- ☐ Regardless of their reaction to your words, sit firm within yourself.

- ☐ Congratulate yourself for taking the first step to speaking your truth.

As time goes by, the process will become easier and easier. Do not anticipate what the other person will say or what their response will be. Communication starts when you open your mouth to voice your words. It is up to them to respond with their energy. Do not argue. Simply say what you need to say. By voicing your truth, communicating without restriction, you will start to open this very important channel of energy. You can become lighter and your chest and vocal chords will become more fluid and alive!

Chapter 6.

THE INTUITIVE ENERGY CENTER

Intuitive Energy

My life is filled with insight, truth, and the vision I have created for my greater understanding

Significance: Utilizing your insight. Hearing your own truth, feelings, and thoughts with clarity. Connection to internal understanding. Feeling strength through the insightful understanding of one's own consciousness and thoughts. Finding the feeling of confidence and comfort in knowing one's truth.

Ability to distinguish the truth and insight of oneself vs. the thoughts and words of others. Standing in confidence with the reality, not the illusion, of one's life.

Balanced: We feel able to make choices and feel inspired and secure with the possibilities of life and its undertakings. We understand that how we live, how we interact in life, and what we bring to our life and relationships is in secure alignment with one's life purpose. Being able to move through the human experience as a secure knowing and insightful being. Accepting oneself and the life that is before and behind us.

Unbalanced: We feel at odds with our feelings, thoughts, and our ability to trust ourselves. Inability to trust others. We can have difficulty with clarity when making decisions and confusion about how to move through life with confidence. We can feel paranoid about those around us and have difficulty concentrating or sleeping with calm and restful hours. A feeling of restlessness, unclear thoughts that cannot come to conclusion, and a sense of imbalance in decision making can be a challenge of the intuitive energy.

༄༅༄༅༄༅༄༅༄༅

The Intuitive Energy Center is often called the "third eye" and is closely linked to our ability to receive and, thereby, *see* outside the realm of this so-called physical reality. It is the conduit to our own insight, intuition, and psychic power.

Intuitive energy is associated with inner knowing. It is an area of our physical body between the eyebrows and moving into the skull. It has an energetic connection to waves of thought and perception and the subtle sensations that we feel within our connection to that energy. If we allow our inner self to hear and feel from this center of consciousness, we experience the *truth* of the matters. This kind of understanding cuts through mind chatter and analytical thinking. Developing and/or understanding this energy center can be a truly enlightened journey.

The Third Eye vs. the Intuitive Energy Center

The Intuitive Energy Center is located between the upper forehead and the center of the eyebrown. There is a strong association of this center with the pineal gland which science and medicine does not yet realize. The pineal gland, energetically, is an area that differentiates between truth and falseness, between clarity and the illusion of dimensional separation. Ultimately, it is the place that has a clear and concise access to infinite awareness and consciousness. This particular gland is of importance for those who wish to understand the intuitive connection associated with or linked to the physical body. It is the direct connection to the feeling sense that alerts the physical body, basically known as the gut feeling.

Why is this area of the body called the "third eye"? In the conscious world, the world of the tangible, our eyes see for us. To see beyond the central vision capacity, we use peripheral vision--and there are: far-peripheral, mid-peripheral, and near-peripheral visions. These various modalities enable us to see areas that are not readily available through the center of our normal vision. They expand our seeing and give us signals that we need to properly address and identify what we see visually and where we are in space. There are also areas outside the so-called normal senses of vision and perception which we know exist but it is very difficult to define within the scientific communities as of date. They know that the brain is receiving signals, but they are not clear on where the signals are coming from and, more importantly, how we receive them. These areas are able to expand our vision and give us signals that we need to properly interpret if we choose to go outside our normal capacity for immediate vision.

Our intuitive energy or insightful energy is associated with our inner spirit. Our inner spirit knows the energy of this tangible material life and life outside of this hemisphere or dimension. It is constantly and consistently connected to it. When we have access to this insightful helper, we can rest more, create in a more peaceful way, and live within the structure of what is useful and brings us happiness.

Have you ever felt like you wanted to make a decision that you did not make? Have you ever known the answer to a question, but went against your own *knowing*? All of us have had the experience of having a strong feeling about what we need to do or say that we often ignore. We over think and lose touch with our inner self, the part of ourselves that is sending signals and senses to protect and assist us.

What would happen if you were able to access, hear, and interact with your intuition more and more? What would it be like if you could just slow your life down, just a tad, to hear yourself? Now, understand that it would not necessarily completely eliminate the sadness or mental and emotional challenges. It may not protect you from *all* of what naturally happens as people grow, experience on-going life, become ill, endure life challenges, and finally pass from this life. These are all crucial experiences that come your way to help you develop into who your spirit knows you are capable of being. But your intuition can, and will, help you connect to yourself and access answers and directions for making life choices that are critical and life changing. The biggest challenge we face with having access to this information is to truly listen.

Many people have asked me about my own unique intuitive ability and how it affects the outcome of my life's lessons. Somehow, they have thought or guessed that my uncommon connection through my gift of insight, leading into the worlds and communities of medicine, science, the environmental studies, professional athletes, entertainers, and successful entrepreneurs, has somehow given me the golden ticket to *escape* the moments and experiences that are not so favorable. The fact is events and experiences happened for a reason; they are important for us to grow. I have had several people, on more than one occasion, say to me: "Why did that happen to you?" Why didn't you "look into it" before it happened to avoid the aftermath? Most people feel that tuning into their intuition will clean their life slate and help them to escape the inevitable moments of life that are painful and uncomfortable. That is not the case, as it would negate the valuable lessons of life, both deemed *good* and *bad*.

Intuition and insight can, and will, help us understand life on a much deeper level. It guides us to making better choices; it helps us experience the moments we desire; and it directs us toward the creation of more of what we want in our life. It supports us to achieve a place of contentment and fruition.

Ultimately, the Intuition Energy Center connects us to our truth and supports us as we move through life's ups and downs, to give us a stronger sense of what is the best for us and those we love.

Intuition is a tool used to gain insight into challenges that might require deeper understanding or to resolve inner conflict when making choices and decisions. If you have ever felt your intuition, that knowing of what is right or any other feeling associated with *knowing*, you will identify with the understanding of this intuitive energy. Regardless of how you interpret it or identify with it, you do know it is there and available if you would like to call on it.

There are many ways to access your inner self, your inner insight. Using intuition and accessing your unique style of insight is a personal process and it can become one of the greatest gifts you give to yourself. Is it imperative that you learn how to use your intuition? Absolutely not. We do not need to access our intuition to create balance in our life or to create prosperity. Insight and intuition are conduits for those who want to take the understanding of feeling, hearing, seeing, and knowing the truth to a very deep core place.

Various Types of Intuition

Many people get confused about where intuition comes from. I have been asked over and over by those seeking to develop their own sense of insight and intuition to describe the difference between the 'feeling' of the body and the mind's 'thought.' For those who do not have an understanding of my gift, I am able to see, hear, feel, and clearly identify energy on all levels. I have been called an "energy master." My gift is directly linked to my mother, Judy Kay, a highly tuned clairvoyant with clairsentience. She is an accomplished woman who has been using her gift professionally for over 40 years. My feeling about intuition is simple. It is an internal core knowing that you have access to, through feeling, seeing, smell, thought and/or hearing. That being said, let me describe it more fully. There are a number of different abilities.

Clairvoyance:

One who "sees" clearly, has a sense of *seeing*. If you are able to sense or see things that are not in the common dimension we all live, you may have clairvoyance. It is a unique gift that you use to go into areas of conscious energy, thoughts, and feelings to explore a reality other than what is readily available to the naked eye. This is the ability to gain information about an object, person, location, or physical event through means other than the known human senses.

Clairsentience:

One who "feels or senses." For instance, if you are in a crowded group and you have a *feeling* that something terrible may happen, just a hunch, and a few minutes later someone falls ill, a falling object hits a person standing near by, or a car accident occurs near by. That is our *senses* alerting us energetically that something is about to occur and causing us to sit up and take notice.

Clairaudience:

One who gains information by hearing and listening to an inner sound. Hearing a tone, sound, voice, or the feeling of hearing, that is unheard by others is considered Clairaudience.

Clairalience:

One who receives information through the sense of smell or taste, just as if it were truly in your immediate environment.

Claircognizance:

Clear knowing--a thought or a knowing that is received through the brain area. Claircognizance means "clear-knowing." For claircognizants, their higher self or spirit guides put information in the form of thought into their mind. This can be a compact load of information that is *downloaded* into the mind. It can be smaller insights about people and situations here and there. It can be an inspired idea.

All claircognizance is characterized by this strong sense of knowing that goes beyond logic. The fact that the intuitive information comes into the mind, not into the heart or the mind's eye, is clearly a mystery to the scientific communities.

Patricia's Story

One of the saddest experiences I endured as both a mother and professional intuitive is Patricia's story. Patricia was living on the East Coast and had a son living on the West Coast while he attended college. As a young adult, he had suffered with drug addiction. This story describes the incredible connection that Patricia had to her son through her intuition, her insightful self.

Many parents seem to have this connection with their children. They know when they are sick, feeling sad, feeling lonely, and need assurance of various sorts. Patricia and Adam share a particularly heart-breaking story.

When Patricia and I discussed her health challenges, what I noticed immediately was the strength of the energy associated with the experience she had endured. The energy that was affecting her physical body was intense and very real. I was nervous for her as she opened up while I accessed her heart energy. Her sense of attachment to her beautiful son was incredible. Every time her son needed help, she could feel it in her heart and her stomach. She knew it and he knew it. It was almost as if they were still connected by the umbilical cord that brought them together from the creation of his life.

It was not always a safe and comfortable feeling for her. When Patricia's son was in high school, he developed an addiction to heroin. This realization shook and collapsed the entire family. When he went through the challenges of drug addiction, Patricia herself developed challenges in her stomach (self-assurance), ulcers, and high blood pressure (love energy). Each time he was able to overcome the illness of addiction, she too became a little stronger physically.

He had been clean and sober for over 18 months when the family agreed that he would attend a university on the West Coast. He was feeling strong, sober, and ready to embark on a wonderful journey with other college students. The only person who would be left behind was his old high school sweetheart, Alecia. They had grown up together. She too had challenges with drug addiction. She was actually the person who introduced Adam to heroin in the ninth grade of high school.

They had not been together for over a year. Adam felt that he was strong enough to move away, be on his own, and become independent and educated--something that was very important to him. He wanted to prove to his mom, especially after everything they had gone through together. He wanted to start over. A fresh start, new relationships, new surroundings.

The first and second semester went very well. He maintained A's and B's in his classes and started to truly enjoy the life away from his parents and the closeness of his new community. He had met new friends, was clean and sober, and started to feel very good about his life and himself. Then, Adam received a phone call from Alecia who wanted to travel to the West coast for a visit. Adam was told that she did not want her parents or his parents to know about the visit. He agreed to keep it a secret.

The following day, Patricia called to check in. She told Adam that she felt he would get a message or phone call from Alecia. Patricia saw Alecia coming to visit and knew that it would not be a good idea. Adam did not want to break the promise he gave to Alecia, so he heard his mom and said he would take precautions if the situation arose.

Two days later Alecia arrived in Northern California. She was a wreck. Adam immediately knew that she was on heroin again. He felt compassion and sadness for her. He took Alecia to his apartment and they talked for hours. It was Thursday, so they took it easy that evening, just hanging around. The following evening, Adam was invited to a huge gathering at the university with bands, booths, and lots of weekend activities. For some reason, Adam started to drink that Friday night and then he and Alecia started to *party* like old times. Little did Adam know that later that evening an event would be put in motion that would change his entire life. His mom tried calling him several times but he put his phone on silent as he did not want her to know that he was drinking and certainly did not want her to know that Alecia was in Berkeley.

At 1:30 am Patricia was in her bed sound asleep. She suddenly bolted up, filled with anxiety and fear, felt a rapid heart beat, and saw the vision of her son calling out for help. She remembered trying not to hyper-ventilate and laid back down to try to gather her thoughts and feelings. She grabbed her phone and immediately called her son. No answer. Within 10 minutes, she received a call from one of Adam's room-mates. Adam had just passed away from an overdose of heroin. They had called an ambulance when they discovered his life threatening challenge, but, sadly, he had already passed away. Alecia flew home the next day, back to her parents. The room-mates disclosed to Patricia that Alecia did in fact arrive in Berkley just a few days earlier, the day after Patricia called Adam to warn him of her intention to visit him.

The day I received the call from Patricia, it had been ten years since the passing of her beloved son. The pain Patricia felt in her heart was as real and alive as if it were yesterday. The reason for her call was to gain information on how to settle and calm this *alive* energy as it was affecting her health in deep ways. As I mentioned earlier, this pain, this agony, this severe suffering had affected her heart, her mind, and it was destroying her health, even though it occurred ten years earlier. We worked together for several weeks. She was able to gain answers to her yearning questions surrounding the life her son had created on his own, as he was doing his very best to step into manhood. Answers, confirmation, and hope were the tools Patricia needed to start her slow recovery from the devastation she felt surrounding her son's very young life and his tragic death. The death she was aware might take place as she desperately called and called to alert her son. The pain she had been holding inside herself for *not being able to save* her beloved young boy almost took her own life. The blood pressure challenges, the anxiety, and the disconnection from the life she so desired to live in all held nicely in an area that was creating severe emotional and physical challenges.

Her story exemplifies that no matter how intuitive you are you cannot change or help another person if they are unable to hear you, take your advice to heart, or take action to change. The good news is today Patricia dedicates herself to helping parents and kids who have addiction issues. She has truly used her life lesson to cultivate a deep connection to her intuition as a way to be of service to others.

Connecting to Insight & Knowing

RECONNECTING WITH YOUR INTUITION AND FEELING

When you can access your inner core intuition, you can, and will, create a life of balanced thoughts, healthy relationships, and the energy necessary to feel and, ultimately, fulfill your deepest desires. The most important part of this exercise is to be completely honest with what you feel and hear. The first feeling, thought, or suggestion you interpret is the truth! Remember, it is not what you *think*. When we process our thought or feeling through the brain, we have lost our ability to feel and see the truth. Why can't we process our intuition through the brain? If it is not stored in your brain from some other conversation, reading, repetition of thought, or experience, how can you possibly obtain the information or insight you desire? Given that what we are trying to access is not our mental energy, it is our intuitive energy which can only be accessed through our feeling. The feeling is what you want to access.

A rule of thumb: if it takes more than a few seconds and you take your energy back up to your brain, *stop!* When I teach the energy of intuition, the first shift I look for after the breathing is the natural habit to go back up to the brain. It is automatic. If you go up to your brain, then just breathe deeply and start over. With practice, you will be able to feel when the energy shifts from your natural gift of intuition (various types outlined above) energy post to your brain. You will learn to quickly rely on your own intuition source and let the brain rest.

Remember, write down the first answer you see/hear or what you feel is coming to you naturally. There are several avenues for intuition to be accessed. Find your gift, your natural ability to *know*. It can be really fun and exciting! This process can happen quite rapidly if you are truly listening and feeling. The more you acknowledge your intuition, the stronger it becomes.

How will you know if it is your mind or your intuition? Believe in your ability! Hear, acknowledge, and repeat. When you are comfortable, interact with your friends by having them ask you questions. Remind yourself to stay in your intuitive energy center and not your mental self or your brain.

When you are ready, sit in a quiet place, and start by relaxing. Do not put pressure on yourself. Remember when you first learned to ride your bike? Or to practice a musical instrument or learn a new sport? Practice makes perfect as they say. Repetition is the key to learning something new. Please take the time to access your personal insight. It can be an asset for those who would like to expand their awareness of the senses available to us.

Ready? Let's get started. Please grab a piece of paper and pen or pencil and a candle. A candle is important to bring in the energy of light. As you have probably noticed, I encourage breathing throughout the book. Breathing and a combination of three. The breath is our tool to access our true inner self, to feel ourself. The combination of three associates with communication. Communication with energy, ourself, and others.

Please tap three times on the top of your head slowly and gently. Then, move to the forehead, please tap three times on the center of the forehead slowly and gently. And now, move to the neck, the front of the neck, please tap three times slowly and gently. Now repeat this sequence two more times. After you have tapped on the Wisdowm Energy Center, the Intuitive Energy Center, and the Communication Energy Center, you are ready to move into the question and answer phase. Tapping on the Wisdom Energy Center allows your personal knowing to engage in connecting to your intuition; the Intuitive Energy Center allows acknowledgement; and the Communication Energy Center assists in delivering the insightful/intuitive information with clarity and truth. You are ready to go and so are your energy centers!

Questions to Connect to Insight and Intuition

Here are a few questions to get you started. Please start to insert your own questions as you go along. You have an idea of what information you want to access. We all do. Use those questions you have already thought of in addition to what I have suggested below:

- What part of my body responds to my natural intuition?
- If I am able to secure my connection to my intuition, what will change in my life?

- What do I want to understand that can help me connect to my inner knowing?

- What would or could create a barrier for me to connect to my insight, my intuition?

- When my body responds naturally to assist me, will I truly acknowledge my personal gift or will I second guess my feelings?

The more you listen and acknowledge, the stronger the connection will be. Acknowledgment is crucial in this process of opening and strengthening your intuition.

When you are with a close friend or someone you trust, you might ask them to ask you a simple question that you would not know the answer to. Before you accept or hear the question, tap on the part of your body that you have learned will be the conduit for your intuitive gift. Breathe deep three times and then ask him or her to communicate the question. In order for you to truly access your intuition, your insight, you must say exactly what you hear or feel initially. The minute you push the energy up to your brain, which is almost automatic if you have not been using your intuition consistently, you will lose the connection to hearing and knowing intuitively. So remember--do not process through your brain. Breathe deeply, accept the question, and then communicate exactly what you see, feel, or hear. Enjoy yourself. It is a lot of fun, especially when you find your rhythm. You will be creating your new website in no time!

Next Level of Building Intuition

Let's take this practice up a notch. The next time you are in front of a person, anyone, while they are talking, take a deep breath. On the exhale, ask yourself *"What does this person really want from me?"* Keep the thought in your mind while you are listening or conversing with the person. Make a mental note of what you felt.

Truthful knowledge is power. You will utilize the information you hear and discover to help you decide on how to move forward with the relationship, the opportunity, the experience, and the moment. When you are able to discern at this level of intuition, life gets less complicated and you can play a more active role in planning and seeing your dreams and choices come through. You also eliminate the unnecessary energy, time, and thought that you might have spent and wasted prior to developing your ability to really intuit what is truly going on. Repeat this often. As you start to believe in your ability, your spirit or core self will expedite the process for you!

Chapter 7.

The Wisdom Energy Center

Crown Energy

My life is created through thoughts of beauty, joy, compassion, thoughtfulness, and love.

Significance: Connection to Creator, Spirit, or God. Believe in higher understanding. Religious connections and belief of humanity. Inspiration, feeling inspired, expressing inspiration to others. Learning about spirituality and how it applies to oneself. Release of old thoughts no longer applicable to one's feelings or thoughts about creation, god, or the connection to one's will or soul.

Believing in the connection to human understanding and a life of purpose or being of service. The understanding of oneself and the world one lives in as with the support of the creator or one's god.

Balanced: We are connected to the reasons associated with life. The fulfillment of life. The ideas and comforts of living. Having balance in our relationships, creating joy and happiness, and sustaining the energy about living each day with gratitude, compassion, and understanding.

Unbalanced: We are closed or shut down to inspiration, possibilities of life, or to others. We can have thoughts of not wanting to live in this world. We experience internal conflicts about life. Uncertainty about life and its purpose. Leaving thoughts and desires in limbo, not being able to move from illusion to reality. False thoughts and desires that could never truly appear as reality, a total disconnect from the reality of one's life. Challenged by the belief of others. Headaches, pain in the upper head area, pituitary challenges, endocrine system imbalances, insensitivity to physical stimulation, and nervous system restlessness, including neurotransmitter challenges along with insomnia, can be associated with a challenge of the wisdom energy.

※※※※※※

The Wisdom Energy Center is associated with our inner self, with the thinking, feeling, and sensing in our head/brain. It is connected with how we process and interpret the information we take in. Although all of the centers are important, the

Wisdom Energy Center is quite significant. It sets the tone, from birth, as to how we create our core belief systems, build patterns and habits, and relate to love, meaning, and work. It is heavily involved in understanding our true life purpose and basically keeping life in perspective.

Wisdom energy is the connection we have to our internal being and sense of self, as well as a connection to our energy associated with free will, free thinking, and the true understanding of one's self. The information traveling through this energy center sets the stage for *interpretation*, *reaction*, and *response* as we move from childhood into and through adulthood. The Wisdom Energy Center is always evolving, open to change, and can renew itself. It also bridges a spiritual connection to the theory and understanding of choice, as well as experience. It processes our thoughts and feelings and brings the necessary insight for us to move through life with ease or with discomfort, which depends upon how different areas of our body, both the physical and the energetic, have been supported or abused through the childhood years.

Wisdom energy is an expression of our intellect running through our core spirit. This is not the mental or intellectual mind I am talking about. Please take a deep breath while continue reading to allow yourself to get out of your mind so you can really absorb the profound power of this energy center.

The Crown of Our Head and the Soft Spot

The Wisdom Energy Center is located at the top of our heads, at the crown. It is here that we connect to energy consciousness from within and without. This may sound quite abstract, but it actually can be explained in a concrete way. At birth, we are born with what is called a "soft spot" on the top of our heads. It is described by the medical community as a place where many bones of the skull have not quite joined, but will meet and fuse over time, to allow for the growth of the brain. If the brain were at its fullest size at birth, it would be a pretty difficult delivery! All of us are very protective of this place on a baby's head.

Why is it soft and open beyond the notion that the brain needs to grow to fill up the skull? This is our Wisdom Energy Center, the place that allows us to be open and connected to the spirit or God Consciousness until we no longer need to access information and insight from where we once came. Have you ever wondered why children have often said, "Mommy and Daddy, I see god."? Or, that they know god and talk to him all the time? This is the energy center that allows us the direct connection to wisdom beyond this lifetime.

We will experience our *senses* through the opening of the crown or wisdom area of the head. It literally takes years for us to build acceptance into the human life we enter into, from the energetic self we were prior to birth. This may upset many of those who do not believe in life after death or reincarnation. I am not proposing to know the answers to any of those questions, thoughts, or concepts. I am clearly stating what I have seen in the Wisdom Energy Center.

My belief is that this area is much slower to close than what science suggests. While it remains open, this sensitive intricate cavity can, and will, absorb the energy of those who surround the babies. Imagine this soft spot absorbing, like a sponge, all the external energy, experiences, exposure, and feelings from the moment of entry into life. Imagine all that they have learned without understanding the human language. I believe this soft spot closes when the human spirit has absorbed the necessary energy to engage in human experience. The seeds from our childhood up to 6 years of age could be planted into our consciousness. This data will be utilized later in our life as we interact with our experience and moments.

Unfortunately, the experience gained unconsciously and without contextual understanding through these early years is also used unawarely to navigate through our human experience in its entirety. Although it is sometimes difficult to believe, many of the painful experiences we traveled through as children have built the foundation of who we are as adults. It was, if you will, a measuring stick to what we want and do not want, to relive or experience, as adults who are with free thinking. I am not suggesting or implying we invited the experiences of childhood that were painful. I am merely stating what I see as an intuitive; the experiences we underwent as children are used later in our life as a tool for understanding. Over time, we are able to adjust and be comfortable in some areas while are challenged in others as we make our way in this human vehicle.

Once the soft spot closes completely, all of the energy from our early childhood: our thoughts, feelings, words, identification with others, and more, is locked into our physical selves. Unless we choose to walk a spiritual path later in life, we are often run or ruled by these old patterns. Choosing a spiritual, religious, or awareness orientation allows us to access and process this information and ultimately feel the effect of this information, thus, having the ability to transform the experiences and moments into understanding, acceptance, and compassion.

But the majority of people grow into adulthood with their early ideas and interpretations of life trapped into their being and their bodies. These sensations, experiences, and emotions that were absorbed through the Crown Energy Center from parents, mentors, teachers, and the environment have lasting effects on the human experience of the traveler. Our inspirations, anger, fears, feeling of ease, or being anxious were introduced and built into our systems during our first years of life. If we believe what was taught, experienced, and understood as real and workable, we travel through life with ease, calmness, and comfort. If we feel we have been challenged by the experiences, teaching, and interactions, we will find ways to open this channel to start the process of implementing our own thoughts, theories, and ideas of what is necessary for us to connect to life our way!

The Beginning of Feeling and Its Challenges

The association of feeling starts from birth. It is clearly defined during childhood and is securely attached to us throughout our lifetime. We find ways to understand ourselves, bring those into our lives that support our experiences, and learn to relieve the stress associated with the experiences. It is a wonderful journey to understand ourselves and where we come from. With the inevitable pain of living and learning, there is a sense of accomplishment when we discover our true inner self. We find that we can participate in life much more than we anticipated or expected. Knowing our inner self allows us to gain the self-respect and confidence necessary to move on with feeling loved, accepted, and comforted. We are at the helm of our ship--not our parents, siblings, or others. We have set sail on our journey of learning, experiencing, and creating the life we desire and know we deserve.

Going back to childhood, let me give you an example of what is stored in this area of our energy self. When we are not able to find the *quick* relief and comfort responding to our cries or need for food or calm as children, this energy can stay with us throughout our lifetime. Although not as intense or sensitive as it was early on, this pattern must be shifted and understood. As an infant, a baby, or a toddler, the souls of these young beings can feel great disconnected if not acknowledged, comforted, and given touch within their immediate reach. They do not know, "This is my mother" or "I am with my father." All they know is, "For some reason, I am not being acknowledged, cuddled, and, most importantly, *comforted.*" I am being ignored! When a child feels or experiences this feeling, it is stored into their memory box. The child does not know what should or should not happen when they cry; he or she only understands what does not happen, feels, and responds to that sensation.

Later in life, when a child or a grown adult cries out or reaches out and a similar experience occurs, this memory box is triggered. It will trigger old senses, old emotions and feelings, that were originally created through the similar stimulations. This is how the interpretation of feelings and emotions are formed and acknowledged within the human spirit or the human self.

The feeling of being ignored, unwanted, or not paid attention to affects our self-assurance, our self-esteem, and our soul essence. Again, we do not know or could not possibly understand what these *verbal words* mean when we are young. It is not until later in life that we connect the words to the feeling associated. So, the feeling is what we associate with all encounters we have. The *feeling* of it is stored and recycled throughout our lifetime. Once the child is picked up and held, if it happens, he or she now has experienced a new sensation. If not repeated often or with repeated consistency, a child will form a deep need to search and find this new found, and lost, sensation, which could become a lifetime search. Yes, people build their lives around finding the affection, touch, and warmth that they received, or missed, earlier. Conversely, a child who did not receive the human touch may turn away from or even discourage through severe emotion, the idea, thought, or event that would create such an opportunity.

Let's say that this child in particular learned that without being aggressive he or she did not receive affection or attention. This child will have *stored* in their mental self what needs to be done to initiate the human affection and touch he or she desperately wants and needs. This created pattern can remain with a person their entire lifetime and can trap them in endless constricting patterns and self-sabotaging habits.

When a child feels suffocated by too much input (coming through their crown or wisdom center), they may have problems breathing, and perhaps even develop asthma. When a child is over-stimulated with too much in-depth information, too many adult content conversations, or too much stress, without the equipment to understand what it all means intellectually, this child can easily develop symptoms of the *inability* to breathe in life or to consume any additional input emotionally or mentally, and might even disconnect their mental self from their emotional self. By having the emotional and mental self shut down, areas of the brain can respond by not being as sharp, quick, calm, or content as needed to interact through normal channels of communication. The child might end up being slow, hyperactive, or diagnosed with something that resembles bi-polar. Simply put, a feeling of being out of sorts.

There are a huge number of very sensitive children these days. That is because there is so much stimulation and so little rest for young ones. When a child receives too much mental and emotional stimulation, they can experience a *disconnection*. When this occurs, the mental self, or mind, can become very wound up. The energy of the child can start to feel very odd and uncertain. Whatever the emotional trigger was, the mind was not able to handle the input. I see this in households where there is heavy verbal abuse or loud noise from consistent arguing or within households of parents who do not recognize the importance that children have to be treated as children.

This does not mean that it is intentional within the family unit. We all know that the family units today are under extreme pressure in all areas. The stress is contagious and the children absorb it and are often overwhelmed by it.

Have you ever watched a child who is in the vehicle of a parent who is running late for work or a commitment and must rush to get them dropped off at a daycare or school? One hand holding a cup of Starbucks and the other trying to put the cell phone down before they cause an accident. If the parent feels this amount of stress in the morning, imagine what the child feels like. There is no judgement in my statement. I am merely stating a fact regarding the level of stress a child feels when a parent is under extreme stressful conditions. The parent knows that within 20 or so minutes, they will be in the parking lot of their employer. A child has no idea what time means, what the next moment will be or feel like, and surely has no idea how to *defuse* what just happened during the morning rush to get to where they were going. A few days or weeks of this level of stress, and you can surely guess where their nervous system is headed. A few years of this, and clearly there are reasons the child is malfunctioning.

This occurs often without the parent/s even realizing what has transpired. They, the parents/caregivers, were doing exactly what they felt was necessary to maintain their life, to support their livelihood. This is doubly difficult and under more distress if it is a single family household. Unfortunately, many children suffer from nervous system disorders, immune disorders, malabsorption challenges, and finally malfunctioning of the neurotransmitters and neurological function as a result. This can happen without any significant indication until they reach the age of entering an education facility. This is when the utter shock comes across the parent/s face. Because life was merely happening around them, they had no idea the level of stress their children endured. Life happens so fast for families today. The stress our society is under is alarming.

Common Energies that Affect the Emotional Self

Let's say every day you come home and your spouse is yelling or complaining about something, always unhappy, or always uneasy about the day, week, or entire relationship. What you might do could be: exit into another area of the house, tune it out, grab a drink or recreational drug, or simply leave the house under duress. This may go on for months or even years before you just leave the relationship. And if you do not leave the relationship, you have probably found ways to self medicate or secure a life outside of the home which provides relief, relaxation, and comfort.

Imagine if you were a child unable to speak, not able to understand words, or understanding words but clearly not able to protect yourself from the energetic stress. Imagine you do not know how to correct the situation or calm down your nervous system. When this happens, and it often does, the crown or Wisdom Energy Center quickly becomes over-stimulated with an excessive amount of energy that now creates imbalances. This imbalance can lead to sleep challenges, skin disorders, hearing and learning disabilities, and more. Just as adults use various methods to relax and reduce the stressors, children also need an outlet, but rarely, if ever, do parents truly understand the damage that is occurring. They truly have no idea that the energy within the family dynamic has created such a dysfunction. They do understand what this level of stress has contributed to their imbalance. Unfortunately, it is very difficult to truly understand unless you are aware of the energetic component to imbalance.

During childhood, if we are over-stimulated or under-stimulated, our body and mind will become imbalances that we then strive to overcome throughout our lifetime. Discovering the core challenges that affected us as children is essential to balancing ourselves as a result of this wisdom energy that flows down and out throughout the other energy centers.

If you feel stress within your home, within your career, or within the relationships that engage with you, your children feel it tenfold. If you feel that you need a walk, a drink, or a cigarette to relax, know that they feel it more intensely than you. It is crucial to build a surrounding of peace and calm for yourself and those around you and to quiet the wisdom energy when it is agitated. Imagine how could we, even as an adult, endure the stress and live through it without any alleviation. Facing internal challenges without the tools to correct or understand the energy that has been stored within the mind, body, and spirit of oneself would be unending devastating!

Learning Lessons from the Past

I believe that we enter the human experience to learn, explore, have fun, and expand our awareness. To create the environment, as adults, that we yearned for as children. We learned from our families, friends, and loved ones, no matter how difficult the lessons were. We learned how to avoid uncomfortable situations by having sustained them in the past. If we grew up in a loud family, we may choose someone who is gentle, or, we choose someone who yells and we learn to leave if it becomes too unbearable. There is wisdom in this life if, and only if, we recognize and accept that we come here to learn. Our family is with us for this duration to support this kind of growth. They teach and they learn from us. And what we hate most in others is often something we need to come to terms with within ourself.

We are all trying to overcome the past. We all want to make sense out of it and re-negotiate what we were open to at the beginning. We came into this life to understand, learn from, and grow from what happened in the beginning of our lives. As we learn to accept the energy of our past, it can now bring us happiness and balance. If we did not have a yelling mom or dad, we might find a mate later in our life who could destroy us from their yelling. If we did not have a mom or dad with an indifferent nature, we may have walked around life without affection. If we did not have love, regardless of how it appeared in our lives, we might not know just how many ways there are to *love* each other. There are no mistakes.

As we get older, we see and start to understand our wisdom. We only know what we know when we know it. Looking back, we can observe that. If we have self-esteem issues, we might have been in a family that seriously challenged our sense of worth. Overcoming life's challenges and growing strength, courage, and forgiveness are part of being here. It is the core of being human. We have to know that we are not just here for a jolly ride. Life experience is the opportunity to first know ourselves and then to ultimately love ourselves and others. It is a path towards love in its most unconditional form.

Bonnie's Story

A young woman came into my office just after graduation from high school. Her mother wanted to understand more about her nervous system disorder. Bonnie was fine under most circumstances, but at times her left arm and hand would tremble without cause. She had undergone MRI's, CAT scans, acupuncture, massage therapy, and other treatments without any clear indication of the core challenge.

This disorder had been a concern from age four. Progressively getting worse as she began middle school and her mother started to search for answers. Years had gone by without any concrete understanding of what the true cause or long term successful treatment might be.

During our first session together, I spoke to Bonnie about any concerns she had that would create a sense of uneasiness within herself. She did not feel that there was anything in her life that caused great upset. She enjoyed friendships, had a boyfriend she was very happy with, and looked forward to college.

My intuition showed me that from a very young age she was involved in an environment that was closely linked to a female who was angry, repressed, and filled with hormonal challenges. I quickly identified this to be her mother. This was not a subject that could easily be brought up without a parent's involvement. It was clear from our first meeting that her mother was not open to returning to that period of her life openly.

So, I took a different approach. I pulled out the tools I love to utilize during my initial consultations. I wanted Bonnie to access her own information, regardless of where she stored it. With her assistance, I knew she could come to understand what provokes this nervous system challenge. As I put the cards on the table, she quickly and excitedly wanted to know what the yellow and purple cards meant. The self-assurance and the wisdom energy cards. I smiled as I started with my simple yet complete explanation.

What she discovered during our time together, as she started to talk about various things that challenge her self-assurance/self-esteem, her arm started to twitch. It was very apparent that the challenges were stuck in the spinal area behind the stomach, upward to the neck and into the back of the neck. The energy channels were all connected.

During other sessions we had together she started to talk about her mothers anger which she did not take personally, because her mom was always under so much pressure, but did admit causing a great deal of stomach pressure and headaches. Her mother was always under so much pressure that she was not able to always express her own physical challenges.

From a young age, she learned to stuff her emotions, fears, and challenges behind a smile because her mom did not have the capacity to change her lifestyle. Everything was difficult. So, as Bonnie went through school, she always felt that everything was difficult and nothing would be or could be smooth and nice. Her feeling about life was: difficult, stressful, without joy, painful, and hard. The complicated part of the story is the deep feelings of love she felt for her mom. She did not blame her mom nor did she feel that her mom was truly directly involved in her physical/emotional challenge.

Within a few weeks, Bonnie and her mother began to realize that the shaking and pain in Bonnie's left arm were closely associated with loud noise associated with anger or stress. When this type of environment was present, Bonnie was not able to control her nervous system, which automatically went into stress mode affecting the nerves in her neck.

Bonnie started to understand where the blockage, stagnation, and trigger was, which began her journey to healing the Wisdom and Self Assurance Energy Centers. With the help of shiatsu, acknowledgment, and staying away from environments that she knew would be disruptive, she is on the road to recovery and strengthen of self.

She has also started to understand that even though her life with her mother was filled with stress, anger, upset, and fear, it was not the life that she needed to have or create for herself. Through this process of learning, her mother also learned that she, too, did not have to carry this burden that was no longer necessary. These two women clearly love each other. Because the energy was not intentional, and her mother had tried for years to help her find answers to this challenge, there was no deception energy that needed to be addressed.

Connecting to Personal Consciousness & Awareness

RECONNECTING WITH WISDOM ENERGY/INNER KNOWLEDGE

The most effective way to connect with the wisdom energy is by acknowledging it exists in the first place! Knowing and understanding that the incredible access we have to our divine self is a gift, and it is primary. All we need are some basic tools to make the leap to give our spirit self more credit than our intellectual self. This shift will create an incredible energy that is often misunderstood and totally under-rated. When you learn to listen to your core self, it is totally different than listening to your mind or brain. Listening to your spirit self is quite an awakening.

Our spirit houses itself within this physical shell and can be touched, embraced, and a partner with us.

Through simple meditation techniques, we can soothe and calm down our entire system from the crown to our feet. When we practice, we are able to allow the free flow of information to figuratively (and others might claim tangibly) re-open the crown for a renewed connection to spirit, God Consciousness, and beyond. This process is gentle but can also almost rocks you from the inside out and the outside in to relieve the pain of the past and re-kindle a new link with the divine.

The head area and the mental area are places that must be kept calm as often as possible. Distractions that are too emotional, mental pressure that is too intense, and environmental issues can cause a great deal of challenge to this area. Take a break often. You need to remind yourself to take a break so that you will learn to keep yourself calm and allow the information and signals coming from your inner wisdom and knowing to soothe you, instead of running you ragged.

The Preparation: I like to create a space that includes gentle music with this daily practice. Music soothes the soul and relaxes the nervous system. Most importantly, it connects us to the energy that can balance our system without any effort. Piano, flute, guitar, and orchestra all provide the notes that coordinate simultaneously with our nervous system. I have a few selections on my website if you need help with useful suggestions. Candles also add a great sense of beauty and peace to this practice.

I recommend a minimum of 10 minutes of practice a day. I prefer 20 minutes but, if you are like most of us, it is not always easy to carve that out. But if you can, please do. You are worth it and your body absolutely needs it. Let's turn your music on and light your candle.

Breathe in a small steady smooth flow of breath, allowing it to move through your lungs and throat slowly. The reason for small breaths is to allow you to focus just a moment on your breath. This is not a heavy breathing exercise. It is meant for nothing more than a moment to acknowledge that you are breathing! Our breath carries us throughout our lifetime and yet we rarely ever stop to recognize how our breath affects us. When we feel anxious we start to breathe slowly to access the healing ability of our body, our natural healing ability. Allow the breath to move through your body as a tool for self-relaxation. Allow the music to flow through your body as you breathe gently and with intention. You can even tell your body and your mind that you are present. Remember, your spirit must find comfort in this physical body.

If it is comfortable for you, I like you to lie down during this practice part. The physical body likes to have a solid foundation for the back area when it is rejuvenating the nervous system. Your music is playing, your back is supported, your candle is lit. You are in your moment.

The Process: Now, think of one thought or area of your body, one of the energy centers you would like to know more about, to relax into. Maybe you want to relax your jaw, the communication energy. Or you want to soothe your nervous system, the intuitive energy, or your mind, the self-assurance energy. You choose.

Now, focus on just one feeling associated with that energy center. Take a breath to commit to make a positive shift of your energy. Access your soul self, your deepest truth by saying out loud: *I am open and readily available to connect to my core self.*

Let's use a simple energy building method to start. Let's feel our breath and recognize that it is attached to our life, our mood, and our communication with ourself and others. Awareness is key to the energy center. You know deep down what you want to shift in your interaction with yourself and others. How then is that possible? Acknowledgment. Remember, the reaction and response to how we interact with others is automatic for most. How many of us have a certain manner at home and a completely different manner at the office or with others? How do we interact with our family when we are not seen by others and our social circle vs. when we are seen by everyone? Let's do our best to bring all the energy of ourself into one self, into one "compartment," not several. This will allow for free flowing energy to be abundant at all times. Compartments can be so confusing, yet we all have created them out of necessity.

Choose a phrase that supports your desire to access what you know deep within, the energy stored in your Wisdom Energy Center. A few suggestions to get started are:

- ☐ My internal knowing is powerful.

- ☐ My knowledge, my truth, is available at any time I choose to access it.

- ☐ I can trust my thoughts, my feelings, my internal insight.

- ☐ I am not afraid to hear myself, to know my truth.

- ☐ I am moving toward understanding more about my internal wisdom.

- ☐ I am able to be a free thinker because I am connected to my personal power and my personal knowledge.

Find your own words by listening to yourself. This is a great way to introduce yourself to your spirit. Allow your spirit to assist you here, it is simply you connecting to you!

Please do not try to figure out how this shift will happen. We all want to. Our mental self wants a tangible. It wants to know how it all *fits* together logically. Do not try to think your way through it. Allow your spirit, your consciousness, and the energy that supports your life to figure it out for you. To be the natural support available to you. Know that your inner self, your inner knowing, has the key to support your happiness and well-being. You must believe it for it to happen. It is much easier than you may think.

Once you have confidence and awareness of this energy center, you will be able to use this energy center to begin the balancing of the other energy centers with your individual insight. Although you can balance the other energy centers one by one without the assistance of this energy center, the connection with the Wisdom Energy Center helps strengthens and accelerates the shifts.

Chapter 8.

Energies That Destroy Hope, Health, and Well-Being

Illusional Energy:

Being truthful with ourself and others is imperative for growth, understanding, and creating what we truly want in our lives. But what I call "illusional energy" is something we humans engage in much of the time. It is truly a waste energy that permeates and contaminates all of the other seven energy centers and can literally make us sick. Yet, it seems to be a common fact of life. I define 'illusional energy' as a creation of experiences or relationships that have been manipulated through one person's dream or intention, but have not been communicated to the other person. This lack of honesty does not allow the other to participate, interact, or engage in the experience. It leads to massive deception, manipulation, and ill-will. Being out of integrity or congruity tears the physical and energetic body apart. Illusional behavior is hurtful and often so abusive that it can change the course of peoples' lives in deeply damaging ways.

The energy utilized through illusional energy can be more than heart breaking. It can utilize large amounts of precious time in the lives of those engaged with the planning, thinking, and anticipation of a dream or intention that has no foundation. The energy associated with this type of thinking or dreaming can be exhausting and can lead to illness, suffering, and mental and spiritual grief. Illusional energy is disappointment (unrealistic, brute), and it, inevitably, backfires. Why do we do this? Why do we create feelings, thoughts, and intentions in our private minds without sharing them with those we seek to connect with?

Human beings are so often run by fear and by not feeling good enough. They fail to admit the honest truth of a situation (which they usually know) because they are afraid of rejection and feel that if they just wait, things will magically work themselves out. Often, we simply long for something so much and we deceive ourselves into believing that if we spill the beans, express ourselves, and speak up too soon (before the perfect moment, in the perfect place), we will lose what we long for. All of this *reasoning* is created solely within the mind of the "planner" without the other person's knowledge. It is a false kind of advertising. The truth is that the dream which leads to disappointment has been created in the person's mind prior to the interaction. By not allowing the other person to have access to the entire truth of the matter, he or she can only respond to the *seen* energy, but not the *unseen* energy. Do you see and feel where the confusion might come in?

Is it clear that the initiator is the person who has created a platform for failure? This person is flying solo. They are in a dialogue that basically, and sadly, does not exist. Yes, certain pieces do exist, the part that has been laid on the table, in some version. The core thought, however, is left off the table. So, there is pain, suffering, confusion, manipulation, and the end result is-- defeat. For both parties.

How many times have we tried to manipulate someone without them knowing it? How many times have we set a relationship or partnership up for failure just by not confiding our intention? No matter how false, many of us hold on and believe that we will obtain our goal, win our battle, and make our private dream come true. So we plan, wait, plan, wait, and finally, almost always, do not achieve the goal. Or, when the plan actually does work out, in some version, the *feeling* behind it is not what we wanted or needed. We expend an enormous amount of energy outlay and almost inevitably end up feeling and getting just the opposite of what we craved. Then, we feel despaired, depressed, useless, and unloved or unaccepted.

I have seen this cycle repeated over and over again. I have worked with many people, both young and old, male and female, who have created in their own mind the scenario they needed to keep their life moving in the direction that has brought them hope, possibilities, and attraction to what they truly desire. Unfortunately, they have not told their partner, or the partner they wish to be with, the entire dream or creation they desire. After weeks, months, and, for many, years, the disappointment starts to build an energy all of its own. The more they strive to obtain their secret goals, the more intense and disastrous the energy between them and the other person becomes. The results are generally horrific, where one partner just does not know what is going on while the other has been carefully calculating their every move. The person involved in the scheme, participating unknowingly, has no way to defend themselves when they almost always come up *empty* in the success part of the relationship or partnership. They are caught off guard and actually have no idea what the *right* response is, from day to day.

Relationships are Built on Trust and Honesty with Yourself First

How do you feel when you have been seemingly taken advantage of? How do you feel when you have found that betrayal was a part of the relationship you felt was so endearing earlier? Be mindful to speak the truth as often as possible. If you are not speaking the truth, not allowing the person you engage with to be able to have free choice to either participate with you or not participate with you, you are taking that which is not yours to take.

Speak the truth as often as possible. Do not waste valuable time and energy on a dream or idea that includes another, who has no idea of your motivation or your need to manipulate them and their reality for your sake. This is not the proper way to create balance within your life. This is creating illusion, which will hold a great deal of emotional challenge and disappointment for you and the other person. And, this illusion will play itself out over and over as the other person in the illusion rarely knows or understands what they have done wrong or what they have done to disappoint or make you feel unhappy.

A scenario that can happen is that the one with a *secret* need does everything they can to get the other person to meet them there, and in the end finds out that it was an empty dream or illusion that took up so much time and energy. This does not even take into account the *pins and needles* of anticipation as they move through the illusion they created and had hoped would be real, day in and day out.

How can the right mate, relationship, career, or emotional tie attract and attach itself to you, if you are not honest and forthright in your desires?

> *When you communicate the truth about your wants and needs to yourself, to life, and to others, there is a kind of alignment that appears. The right person or experience often shows up to accommodate you and what you desire.*

Sandy's Story of Illusional Energy and Disappointment

Sandy was a young woman in her early twenties who was beautiful, well spoken, and bright. She had set an intention to *land* a husband to fulfill her fantasy of immediately having three children to make her life complete. Sandy did not share this dream (demand) with Doug, her soon to be husband, nor did she mention it to him after the wedding. She had a lot of confidence in herself, along with a persistent personality, about how to get what she wanted. Doug, the innocent bystander, walked into Sandy's big plan without the knowledge necessary to either support her vision or protect himself, his emotional balance, or his financial goals, if he felt otherwise.

The first year of their marriage was uneventful. Doug told her many times that his desire was to purchase a home, accumulate savings, and 3 to 5 years down the road plan for a family. He did not want to bring children into the world without a substantial platform to build from. His father had lost his employment when Doug was a young man and the family felt incredible despair and loss because of it. Those youthful years were filled with memories of sadness, often directed towards his dad, and ultimately deep grief for his mother. His dad did his very best to find odd jobs, but in their small hometown it was very difficult. So Doug's mother had to try to earn money as well. This created a great deal of stress and strain.

Doug was very certain that children would not be welcomed until he had established a life of comfort, stability, and steady income. Again, he had confided to Sandy about this plan early on in their marriage. Sandy, although listening but not *hearing*, felt that her secret plan of having children and being a stay at home mom and wife would truly create happiness. She realized that she was at odds with Doug's ideas, but she felt that he did not really understand how great things could be if he simply participated in her dream.

The second year of the marriage, Sandy stopped taking birth control pills, despite the fears and real stress Doug felt about having children early on in the marriage. She felt that if she were happy, Doug would surely be happy for her. Three months later Sandy became pregnant. She could not wait to tell her husband and rushed to his office to communicate her fabulous news. At last, her dream was at her fingertips. When she sat down in Doug's office beaming with joy, she could barely contain her enthusiasm. He sat down wondering why his wife was so excited. Without thinking of Doug's needs and feelings, his numerous conversations about children, and his stress from childhood, she blurted out, "Guess what, honey? We're pregnant!"

Doug felt sudden shock. His stomach and chest contracted. His eyes filled with tears and he could not find the words to express himself. Doug finally choked out the words, "Really, are you sure, honey?"

"Oh yes, I just got the results. Aren't you excited? I am so excited, finally. Finally, the family *we* have always wanted!" Her words echoed into his ears, heart, and his entire being. He held back the tears of disbelief, sorrow, and fear and stood up to embrace her. She was so filled with her own joy and the elated feeling of bliss that she did not see, feel, or sense the emotional collapse her husband was going through. Sandy left the office as quickly as she rushed in. Doug fell into his chair and felt totally numb. He was lifeless, as though his entire world had just caved in.

Later, Sandy spent the entire day planning her *illusion* of just how wonderful things would be now that she was with child. Doug learned a lot that evening. Sandy had her *list* of how things would develop over the next 7 months. She had jotted down all the important details including their participation in classes, the purchases that needed to be made, the doctors' appointments he had to go to, and on and on. In her own mind, Sandy created the perfect vision for *her* family, which includes her husband's responses and participation.

That night, when they went up to bed, Sandy was very persuasive and sexual, and intent on making love. She was so filled with herself and her connection to her womanhood that she made it clear that it was a night to celebrate. Unfortunately for Doug, all these emotion and conflict were over-whelming. The truth is both individuals were experiencing deeply rooted feelings that are completely opposite. For the first time in their relationship, Doug was defeated, without any sense of feeling in his lower extremities. Sandy was crushed and humiliated and became quite agitated. She cried endlessly. Her words were damning and hurtful: "Why can't you be happy for us?" "What is wrong with you? This is the happiest day of our life!" "It's all we need to complete our family!" "Don't you love me? Don't you want our baby?" "Is there someone else?"

Doug just laid in bed in disbelief. What had happened? What was going to happen? Doug was not in the place mentally to answer any questions in his own mind, let alone try to express himself to his wife. Tomorrow may bring a brighter feeling is all Doug thought.

As weeks and months passed, Doug was not able to ignite intimacy with his wife on his own. He spoke to a friend of his, who suggested he see a physician to seek professional help, and began treatment for erectile disorder. He was able to start making love to his wife after taking a prescription medication. Sandy was not aware of the challenge Doug was having. Sandy was in her own world preparing for her baby.

Life for Doug changed the day his wife stepped into his office with her joyful news. When he found out that she stopped taking the birth control that they both agreed upon about the pregnancy, and the *list* of what Doug *must* participate in to become a well-respected father and husband, the love was lost. Sandy was the only person who was not aware. The months passed by quicker than Doug had expected. Work was very busy and Sandy was equally as busy with her plans. Doug started to meet with his buddy from work more often, sharing his emotions with someone he trusted. He started to drink a bit more than usual. It helped take the edge off just prior to stepping into Sandy's world.

Doug's son arrived a few weeks early. Sandy was in heaven. She could not be happier. Doug could not connect to their son. Although he held him in his arms, Doug was filled with enormous pain and suffering. *His dream* of preparing for his children had disappeared entirely.

Several months after their first son was born, Sandy, without thinking, spurted out "I can't wait to have our next!" Doug's heart dropped into his chest. He had severe chest pain travel across his arms, chest, and throat. Within a few weeks, Doug set an appointment to have a vasectomy. His friend from work, Marc, accompanied him. After the procedure, Doug drove home as if nothing had happened.

Three to four times a week Sandy created the *right* atmosphere for Doug's arousal at bedtime. Although Doug willingly participated in the sexual experience, for himself at times and for Sandy, he was never going to participate in being manipulated by her again. Sandy started to become agitated as time went by. No pregnancy. She would have Doug come home from work at a certain time when ovulation occurred but did not share with him that she was busy planning to conceive. Eventually, Doug became hyper vigilant and learned to be one step ahead of his wife, watching and listening to her every move. He felt less and less love and Sandy became increasingly depressed and angry each month that passed by without the great news of her next pregnancy.

Doug and Sandy's son started pre-school. Meanwhile Sandy was anxious. She could not figure out why she had not become pregnant. She was upset that her son was already 4 and that he would be in elementary school quite soon without a sibling in sight. What had happened to her big plan? Sandy was soon in the office of her physician asking for help to handle her anxiety and depression. She sat down one day and confided with Doug. She talked about her *need* to have another child, to ask if he would *please* participate by financing a fertility doctor.

Doug finally told Sandy the truth. He confessed that 3 1/2 years prior, he had consulted with a doctor and decided to have a vasectomy to protect himself from further manipulation. He felt excluded from the partnership and felt she had deceived him. Sandy was shocked and became very angry. She started screaming and became violent, throwing things. Doug had to leave the room. Her anger included insulting and calling him degrading names that were not acceptable to him.

Sandy finally calmed herself down enough to sit with Doug again. They discussed the real issue, Sandy's lies, deception, and her belief that her dream had been more important than the concerns and plans Doug had voiced regarding his goals for his family, including that of his children. Their marriage ended shortly after this disclosure, the result of years of illusional energy gone wild, on both sides now. Neither could trust the other. Ultimately, both had secretly also manipulated the other and created great distress, disappointment, and despair.

If Sandy would have been honest with Doug about wanting children right away they could have gone their separate ways early on. Doug would have found a woman who was a planner, a woman who could *hear* his desires. Sandy could have found a man who, like herself, wanted to start a family immediately. Our life's path does include all those who want to participate with us in our dreams and desires. If we do not call upon them with our truth, how will they find us?

Communicate Your Truth!

RE-CONSTRUCTING HONESTY AND BALANCE

Please have a pen and paper handy. Now sit quietly with eyes closed. Breathe in three times, slowly, and then softly ask yourself the following questions out loud. Listen for an answer. When you hear your honest truth, open your eyes and write down your words.

- ☐ What am I trying to create in my life that is out of balance?

- ☐ What am I really trying to gain in my relationship with ...., without his/her awareness?
- ☐ What do I need to be honest with in regards to my relationship with ....?
- ☐ How much energy will I have available to me if I live in truth?
- ☐ What is the reason that makes me feel I cannot be honest with those in my life today?
- ☐ Creating a sense of balance starts with me and my intention with ....?

Now read your answers back to yourself out loud. Please listen to your answers. Are they true? In order to really be in balance within your inner self, you must know what you really want from your surroundings, your environment, and those that you feel are in your life for support, affection, love, and comfort.

Remember, this is about *you!* This is not a technique to bring in the energy, thoughts, or needs of anyone but you. Do not confuse yourself with what is expected or needed from you. What do you truly want? What do you truly need to create a sense of balance, excitement, joy, and comfort in your life? How can you interact in an honest and truthful manner with those you have surrounded yourself with?

EXPECTATION ENERGY:

Expectation energy is the destructive energy that sweeps away hope, love, contentment, and happiness. Expectation energy becomes so focused that the reality of the relationships, the essence of the relationships, and the affection of the relationships, even with oneself, are destroyed. If you only had one moment, one single moment, with a special person in your life to embrace, to hold, and to communicate all the things you truly feel and want to say, would it be filled with all the expectations, disappointments, and demands?

If you only had that moment, that last moment, with yourself or a loved one, how would you embrace him or her? Would you say the things that you really wanted to say? Could you express your true inner feelings? Would you really want to express all the feelings at the bottom of the anger, pain, and sadness? Or, would you want to spend the *moment* telling them just how wonderful they are, or something about their special place in your heart and in your life? Believe that *any* moment could be *that* moment and start to embrace those you love and care for.

Over the years, I have seen the turbulence and chronic pain in those who have needed to endure the pain associated with regret or attached to *wanting it to be different*. Unfortunately, once we step past *the point of no return*, we have lost the once loving, compassionate, and true heart felt connection that once lived within the two parties; the disconnection has occurred and there really is no return. Even if the individuals come together at a later date, the *feeling* is never really the same. And, for those who will never have the opportunity to come together again, for various reasons, the gap and gouge can be quite destructive. There are many people who live with regret, sadness, and the pain of not being able to communicate to those who have been in their lives, those who have held significant meaning. Reminding themselves often of the words and expressions of feelings they desperately want to communicate, but know it will never be. Have you ever noticed in your own relationships that when the *feeling* is over, it is simply over? Something was said, done, or displayed that broke the special bond that had such high hope, such deep affection and meaning.

Expectation that Kills Love, Relationship, and Integrity

Where do we find the expectation that we project onto others? Where do we find within ourselves the outline, the list or the "play list," of what we need from others to be accepted into our life, our intimate world?

For me, for many years, it was the shoes someone wore. It is an odd thing to say and even more odd to live it. For some reason, I equated success with a person's shoes. Today I do my very best to not look down when I meet someone. It is not a pattern that can be changed easily. Many great experiences could have been mine if I had not had the stubborn idea that without the *proper* shoes, you did not fit in! A huge mistake on my part.

There are many examples of expectation. There are many different ways we communicate expectation: we do it verbally, visually, in writing, non-verbal expressions, and more. It often begins with *illusional* energy and it transforms into *expectation* energy.

During many of my sessions, I suggest that the participants jot down their expectations of their relationship, marriage, children, and leaders in their workplace. It can be quite a shock to those who are not aware of just how demanding and insensitive their expectations are and have been. It can create total collapse and destruction in others.

How many times have you wanted to *take back* or *retrace* what went wrong in a relationship? Each relationship challenge that I have worked with has had one common complaint: *my expectation was not met*. The person was not able to communicate this truth initially. It took them looking inside themselves to find out what really went wrong--the unmet expectation led to the collapse of the relationship. Why do we feel that we have the right to *demand* so much from those in our life? Where does that need and self-righteous behavior come from? To belittle, control, and basically humiliate those who come to assist, love, and protect? Although it is almost always unintentional, the energy behind it is very constant.

When we have a sense of *entitlement* in our life, we feel that we have the right to demand from others. If our demands are met, or will soon be met, we then feel *right* to continue on with the relationships we are engaged in. When they are not met, are not realized, or are not felt, we feel that we must pressure the other participant to meet our demands, or their life will be filled with anxiety, stress, and a feeling of unworthiness.

I have met with several parents who would not allow their child to express themselves unless their expression was that of what was expected. When the parental expectation was not met, the child then became *less than* the person they truly are.

Laundry List of Expectations that Destroy Marriages for Women

Over the years, I have worked with many women. The larger percentage of my work is with women. This next part of expectation energy will focus on women and their expectations. If you are a woman who has had challenges in your marriage or relationships or has female children, this section may be of particular interest to you. My editor and dear friend asked me, "Why focus on the women's expectations?" It can be misunderstood or felt as a *dig* against women. For one reason, and one reason only, this section I have created is to assist women. To help them, if it applies to you, in addressing deep seeded issues surrounding expectations and how they can, and will, destroy happiness and the possibility of successful family units.

Woman is the forefront of the family's success! One of the biggest challenges I face in my work is with the expectation energy from women. Women who need what they need and will accept nothing less become completely imbalanced within their life because of their needs that are not *fulfilled* by their partners, husbands, or children. Those needs have caused the biggest conflict between themselves and those they truly love the most. Women tell me that they need men to be exactly what they want and they withhold when those expectations are not being met, resulting in dangerous implications that can at times destroy the very foundation that must be built. It is not until the marriage has failed and the intimacy is gone that they finally understand just how difficult it was to *achieve* all that was expected. This expectation energy is the underlying *secret* energy of the marriage or committed relationship. Below are the example lists of women's expectation.

List #1 (either communicated or implied without communication) I expect my man to:

- Make enough money to pay the bills.
- Make enough money to pay my credit cards.
- Make enough money to allow for holidays.
- Make enough money to allow for new automobiles.
- Make enough money for dining out.
- Make enough money for necessities and non necessities.
- Make enough money to take care of the children and their needs.
- And, do not make me work if I do not want to, be a man.

List #2 (either communicated or implied without communication) I also expect my man to also:

- Listen to me on a daily basis and really *hear* me.
- Pay special attention to me daily.
- Let me know how important I am often.
- Be my friend.
- Know me, the real me.

- Love me, the way I need to be loved.
- Accept me, regardless of my appearance, mood, or expectations.
- Make me happy.
- Accept full responsibility for our children as I do.
- Do not go out after work if I need you at home.
- Do not take your job more seriously than our family or me.
- Spend any excess time you have at home with me and/or the kids.
- Do not spend money on anything without my approval.

For all the women who are offended by this information, please accept my sincere apology. The lists are for those who have expectations that could be harming the very essences of their happiness and the success of their family. To assist you in understanding how to create a sense of balance, joy, and comfort in your life, I have gathered information from what I see in relationship of those who have come to me for clarity. To learn the reason their relationships are not working. If you are involved in this type of expectation energy, please review what is important in your life. Reflect on the energy attached to these expectations. Realize your intention, realize the feelings you have for your spouse or lover, and move forward according to your heart. Expectations take away the breath of a relationship.

Men and women have two very distinct energies. Men and women are very different in how they process and how they communicate in their personal world. When men cannot *fix* the situation at home, they become very frustrated and agitated. Men want to fix a problem and move on. For most, success depends on men having the answers for their career and their mate, the woman they love.

Women want to discuss, interact, have affection, and communicate their opinions, as a species. Energetically, women attracted to and need the inter-action. Most men do not. Men like to understand what needs to be done and they want to decide, on their own, how to accomplish a successful outcome, and be done. When men realize that these (expectations above) are the expectations that *must be met* in order to live in harmony with their girl friends, spouses, or lovers, the intimacy, success, and dreams stop.

The relationship then takes on a new sense of energy, and urgency, that of *survival*. The once loving and affectionate woman of their dreams, or the women they met and fell in love with, soon becomes their worst enemy, a nightmare, the energy they fight with until they can no longer fight anymore. The disconnection quickly occurs. They either leave, find comfort elsewhere, or become increasingly despondent. This is the beginning of the imbalance of passion energy, stability energy, and communication energy. If these areas are not put back in balance, despair, depression, and lack of engagement in life will occur. Men will keep pressing on because it is expected. But without the joy and passion necessary to maintain success within and without, the energy will quickly disperse.

Because of the amount of pressure we feel in life, no one has *down time*. No one has a minute to breathe, so we shove all the responsibility we feel on to those closest to us. We forget that they too are experiencing that same feeling of being overwhelmed. We start to live in our own little world of stress and unhappiness. Instead of seeing the person as an asset, a support, we start to see them as the person who either makes or breaks our success. The battle begins.

The expectation may never be met. Men do try. They believe that if they can just *be better* at being a husband, a boyfriend, or a partner, then everything will be ok. They believe that if they can just *make it happen*, their wife, partner, or lover will return to be the love of their life.

Unfortunately, it does not happen as often as you might think. As a matter of fact, it may never happen. Men are not energetically wired to handle the energetic responsibilities of the female emotional energy. It is a difficult task for them, even though they truly want to.

Men are very basic creatures. Although some may want to argue this point, from my perspective energetically I see that men have 4 basic needs: food, sleep, work, and intimacy/sexual activity. Family is important to most men but there is a lot of pressure behind creating a family and the responsibilities of children. If they are able to have those four comforts, they will be in their element. If they are not allowed these basic energetic functions, their lives will quickly become very unbalanced. The passion energy, communication energy, and the stability energy will start to feel stagnant. At times, for many men, they never regain their energetic strength unless they change partners.

Men want to make their woman happy. Unfortunately, almost always, they just do not know how.

The energy between men and women is an interesting interaction. The follow up book to The Energy of Life is: The Energy Between Men and Women. To understand the energy that motivates and destroys love, respect, and hope between men and women, it must be understood how each operates as individuals and the difference in the energy shift as they cohabit and agree to accept the journey of becoming one, in unity. It is an interesting understanding that may just surprise you!

Connie's Story

Connie and her husband Stan came to see me. Connie had made the appointment for Stan since he had just learned that he had cancer. She wanted to know what the energy association was that led to his cancer. Her friend told her about my work and they lived just a few streets from my office.

She wanted it fixed *right away*. Connie sat down and was a non-stop talker. After 5 minutes of intense listening, I finally disconnected my engagement from Connie and watched Stan for a brief moment. He sat expressionless, just staring into space. For a moment, I went into his energy to find out what he was feeling. I could hear his mind repeating these thoughts: "Please slow down. Please be quiet. Please stop talking."

I brought my energy back to Connie, who hadn't come up for air. As she continued, I waited for a moment to jump in, and I mean *jump in*, before she went off on some other tangent. I asked Connie if I could speak to Stan for a moment. She caught herself, without much consciousness, and very superficially said, "Oh sure, Jennifer."

So I took the moment to breathe in, asked Stan to breathe in and asked Connie to also take a deep, deep breath. As I directed my words towards Stan, within thirty seconds, Connie butted in, did not excuse herself, and gave her version of the answer. I watched Stan as he closed his mouth, lost his voice, and sat back into the chair with the same blank expression he had moments ago. His eyes met mine a few times during the 30 minutes of ongoing chatter from his wife. We met for a second, he smiled a very gentle smile and, as quickly as that meeting of the eyes took place, his eyes were somewhere else.

While Connie sat chattering, I wondered how long ago Stan had tuned Connie out. Equally a concern, how long ago Connie stopped engaging in the reality of the relationship with her husband.

Connie could not help herself. I attempted a joke when I asked, "Connie, how long have you been talking for Stan?" She started laughing and said, "Since the day we got married."

She went on to say that Stan did not *get to the point* as quickly as she could, so she took the lead years ago. At that very moment, I saw Stan's stomach cringe. At that very instant, I understood everything. Stan had stomach and liver cancer. The stomach cancer had spread to the liver. Connie needed her husband to survive. They had been married for 30 years. She was not going to *allow* Stan to leave her. No, sir! She was going to find a way to *cure* her husband's cancer.

Unfortunately, Stan and Connie could not even agree on what food would be appropriate for Stan during his healing period. Connie was not going to allow Stan to eat the food he loved. Even though he loved it and it was not dangerous, Connie felt that her diet would be best for him.

After our session, I looked Stan directly in the eyes and asked him this very pointed question: "Stan, is there anything I can help you with today?" He stared back at me, raised a bit of a smile from his lips, and, with just a bit of emotion, gently said "No, Jennifer." While he talked, I searched his energy field to accurately hear and see what Stan was really saying. I could hear his emotions repeating the same words, "God, please let me go now." "God, please let me go now."

Stan had lost control of his personal life. Connie's energy had totally consumed him. He was the Vice President of a popular company in town. To see him interacting in this manner was very disheartening. A proud man with such a great reputation did not have a voice within the environment where he lived with his wife. I wondered how this well respected man in our community had lost his core self to this woman's energy. I wondered why Connie needed to belittle her husband. I wondered why Stan did not stand up for himself. And, I thought, why didn't Stan consider a life without Connie?

I do know that once a strong sense of disconnection energy sets in, it is very difficult to bring your spirit back to a place of wanting to try. I see this in those whose crown energy is no longer open or available for possibilities or hopefulness. That is a direct indication that the person may be choosing to leave this world. Sadly, within 7 months, Stan passed away. There is no question in my mind that Stan is resting in peace, finally.

Please do your very best to see all the great and special qualities of those intimate people and circumstances in your life.

Please do not need them to change. *Accept them.* Try to see them as they are right now, their core real self, and love that. Love that at this very moment. Because, the truth is, you really have no idea when the moment will be that you will not have that opportunity. Deep down, I believe that we want to love those in our life. Deep down, it can be a reflection of our own inner needs that must change, and not the others. Acceptance creates an immediate sense of balance, even though it can be difficult at first. Acceptance, while maintaining strong boundary, allows everyone to participate at the level of life they are able to, at any given moment. We are all growing, experiencing, and trying to do our best to be our best. Even though, for some, it does not appear to come as quickly as we would like, we are not here to judge or alienate them because of the shortcomings we feel are affecting them and us.

Feel and Enjoy Each Moment!

REDUCING EXPECTATION ENERGY THROUGH ACCEPTANCE

This is a three-part journal process.

Part 1: Make a list of the people who you currently interact with in your life. What are your expectations with those participants in your life? Please write down what you really expect from these people. Do not edit. Put down your notion of what you get currently. Be bold. Use the technique you learned to access your truth, your intuition. Breathe in a few times before you ask yourself the question. This will override your *mental* reasoning, cutting to the bottom line rather quickly.

As you write your answers, consider the following questions to stimulate your thoughts:

- ☐ Do your children need to meet certain expectations for you in your community or within your family or your social circle?
- ☐ Does your husband need to keep up with the other *neighborhood* men?
- ☐ Does your job need to be as spectacular, meaningful, and elite as your friends?
- ☐ What do you really expect from your: husband, wife, partner, children, family members, boss or leader at work, friends?

Part 2: Now ask yourself:

- ☐ Why are the people in my life *in my life*?

Write down what comes up first. Look for the reason the people in your life are there. Acknowledge the truth about what your relationships are. Find within what you can do to create harmony in the relationships that you already have. Or, be truthful about why those in your life are there, even though the energy of the relationship/s is overwhelming.

Part 3: Now ask yourself:

- What can I do to engage with those I care about without expectation?
- How would things be different?
- How would I act/feel differently inside and out?
- How would I participate in the life of those I love by using supportive and encouraging words and expressions?

Energy starts with you. Determine through your truth and honesty within why you demand and need the people in your life to create success for you. Personal success comes from within. Re-evaluate your relationship with those in your life. Take time each day to confirm why they are there and why you want them to be there. If you do not want certain individuals in your life, gain the courage to release the engagement you have with them. Take baby steps. They are in your life for a reason. When you have learned what you need from the relationship, be prepared to disengage when it is time. You will feel healthier, and so will they.

Be mindful during each day that life is only a moment. Remember, at any moment, things can change so dramatically. Cuddle with those you truly love. Communicate your truth with those you really care for. Get to really know others and allow them to get to know you.

Do you realize, truly realize, that life is a brief moment? Life is a gift. I know many people who are stuck in the past, the pain, the disappointment, the unfairness of life. To those, I simply want to communicate that the clock is ticking. Yes, it will be over soon--the pain, agony, sadness, frustration, and with that, on the other side of that truth, so is the time you have to enjoy what you do have in your life. Those who love you, those who enjoy you, the opportunities you would find if you shifted the energy of those past pains. And, what you have created or can create for the future. I encourage you to look around at those in your life today. Take a deep breath. Look at those you love. Those you are connected with. Even the person you see each morning who you greet with a smile that you may never know further or deeper than that instant greeting. Two humans greeting each other with a smile, a nod, an eye contact that 'Yes, I see you,' I am acknowledging you! Feel them. Acknowledge them. They, just as with you, will not be here forever. Life is just a moment. Enjoy it as often as you can!

STORY ENERGY:

"Story" energy is primarily based on past anger, regret, disappointment, pain, and despair. It becomes an energetic loop that is relived years after years, slowly killing any possibility of happiness. It comes from feeling a lack of closure or resolution related to dramas/traumas and disappointments in your life that did not feel complete. People are haunted by their stories. How many times have you rehashed *your story* in your mind? How many times has your story affected your attitude, energy, and prospects for the future? How many times have you told your story and wondered *why* do I keep repeating myself? This energy dominates your mind and can become an obsessive cycle that runs your life. If your story has no sense of resolve or conclusion, it can even stick in your mind with more force. Do you know anyone in your life who continuously tells their story? Have you ever wondered why a loved one just cannot quite get over the trauma or painful event from the past or why you cannot seem to get through to the person who is *stuck*?

What is the Problem with Story Energy?

Story energy takes the very breath and possibilities of the *now* and *future* moment away from us. It takes away the energy we need to create passion, excitement, dreams, and possibilities for the now and the future. When we have used a large amount of energy first thing in the morning rehashing or worrying over past events, we have diminished the energy and feelings to create what we truly desire.

View the chart below; notice how the energy/resource/capacity we have available each day could be spent. If you have used 50-75% of the energy available to you upon waking with thoughts of mental and emotional pressure, day after day, month after month, and possibly even year after year, how can you function with the heaviness of your energetic challenges and the day ahead? Can you possibly access or utilize the energy you need to operate on a daily basis with optimal energy, hope, enthusiasm, or optimism? The answer is *no!*

Energy Resource Availability/Consumption Chart

Today's challenges:
- financial stress
- health issues
- relationship
- children
- work
- etc.

Past challenges:
- painful memories/stories

Energy left available as nurturing resources: motivation/planning, or to be used for growth

Story Energy Creates Exhaustion

When we wake up first thing in the morning to the same energy that exhausted us the day before, the cycle can begin to take on a *pattern*. We create each day from what we feel first thing each morning. Depending upon our sleep level, our responsibility level, and the lack of or abundance of *passion* in our life, our daily energy is directly attached to what we think and feel. As the pattern becomes embedded in our psyche, the story energy gains momentum. After 27-30 days, if it is repeated through an emotional or mental connection, it will become a strong habit.

Please take a moment and define for yourself the story energy you hold or that holds you within your own daily life.

What challenges do you feel occupy most of your mental and emotional space? What percentage of your day is unintentionally, mentally or emotionally, devoted to: relationship challenges, children challenges, financial worry, past pain, disappointment, despair, career challenges, etc.?

Imagine for a moment that the circle below is the energy available to you as your energy source on a daily basis. Write down your personal ongoing daily challenges. Then chart them out in the circle. Be as honest as you can. Put a percentage next to the areas so you see where you truly stand.

With this information, you can start to change the amount of time and energy you spend in the past. Living in the past does not allow for embracing the future. Find your stressors and then locate the energy center associated with that challenge. Do the exercise at the end of the chapter of that energy center to start to balance that area of your life *right now*.

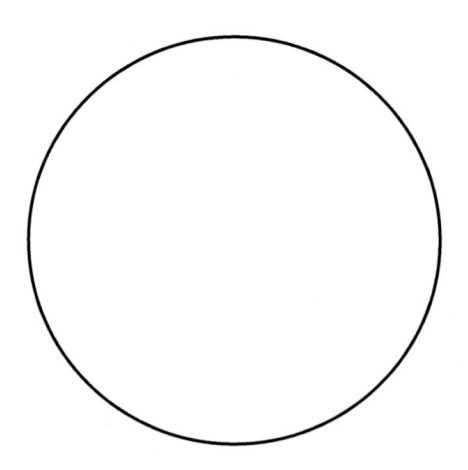

Your personal energy resource chart

Jenny's Story

A young woman came into my office worrying about her mental stability. She was experiencing challenges resulting from a turbulent short marriage, pregnancy later in life, and the abuse of her daughter during the marriage.

When we first sat down, the tears were endless, as were the stories of despair, anger, and helpless feelings. When Jenny met her soon to be husband, Paul, she was in her mid 30's. She was a strong, successful business woman. She was traveled and expressed a great sense of accomplishment and purpose in her life.

Several months after meeting Paul, Jenny became pregnant. Prior to the pregnancy there was very little intimacy between them. They were just getting to know each other, exploring their ideas of feelings, possibilities, and what each other wanted for the future. Finding out that she was pregnant came as quite a surprise. Jenny was already at the age she felt she wanted to slow things down in her life. She had a daughter from a previous marriage who was already 12 years of age. The shock of the pregnancy set the energy in motion for a downslide. She was just not aware of how far down she would slide.

She decided to marry and just get on with the next phase of her life without much consideration. She moved forward with the hope of building a new life, but no planning whatsoever. Just forward movement. Paul did not believe that he could conceive a child, so he was dealing with very different emotions from Jenny. He was caught in the surprise of a lifetime. With his Catholic upbringing, marriage was the answer. They moved on together.

Paul had never been married. In his mid 40's, he was just starting a new professional career filled with possibilities. Because Jenny had been financially successful for most of her adult life, she did not consider that her new husband had not enjoyed the same financial independence she had become accustomed to on her own. She did not understand how to integrate the difference between her reality of finances and his reality of finances. This took a major toll in their relationship.

Soon into the marriage, the walls started to cave in. She had not thought about Paul's student loans, lack of real income, or the behavior patterns she was learning to interact with, while trying to embrace her new pregnancy. The entire, stable platform that she had beneath her prior to this year was sinking quickly. The feeling of not being able to hold onto anything reasonably familiar or of comfort started to create a sense of total imbalance.

During the first few months of the marriage, Jenny became increasingly aware of Paul's roaming eyes. His comments to waitresses, clerks, and neighbors soon became a re-occurring incident that caused great challenges with their intimacy. Paul denied that it was happening, but Jenny knew it was. Not a great feeling when you are gaining weight and feeling a sense of despair and fear as you move into the unknown with a person you barely know.

It was not long before the baby was born. The new family was not connecting at all. There was no stability. The first born daughter, now 13, grew further and further away from her mother as the new infant required every ounce of energy that Jenny had to give. The most important person in Jenny's life, her treasure, was slipping through her hands like sand. She was not able to give any more of herself than the energy she desperately needed to give to her young son. Her daughter knew this intellectually, but the pain was still felt deep inside. Jenny and her daughter were once an unstoppable team. They did everything together. Because Paul had never been in a live-in or committed relationship in his adult life, this was all new to him. He was used to being in charge of his life, participating only as he desired, and pushed on to create his life outside of the family unit, just as he had prior to the marriage and new child.

After the first year, Jenny found out that her finances had been diminished. She became increasingly aware that her limited monthly income, which was reduced when she could not work full time or concentrate because of fatigue and sadness, could not cover the monthly expenses. Paul was not capable of covering the minimal family expenses. His stress began to grow as did his life outside the family unit. She began to feel desperate regarding finances. The once very successful, young woman was not able to see any light at the end of the deep, dark tunnel she found herself in. It was the first time in over two decades that she had to concentrate on two factors regarding income: consistently generated income and necessity spending. One of her deepest fears from childhood of not having enough is, shockingly, here now in her adult life. She was married to a man she barely knew, in a relationship that was never solid or of any pleasure and joy, and with a brand new baby. She loved and adored her new son, but also needed desperately to reconnect with her beautiful daughter whom she missed desperately. The financial obligations were piling up with no relief in sight while the closeness she had felt with her daughter was slipping away. The depression was enormous. The mental, emotional, and physical abuse created a deep sense of despair within herself and her family unit. Decisions needed to be made.

Within 24 months the marriage was over. In truth, the marriage never was. Jenny borrowed money to take her two children to a new home, to start the long journey to healing. Supported by loving friends and her mother, she began trying to put her life back together. As she finished her story sitting across from me, I thought, based upon her energetic connection to this story, that it was just months into her separation. But when I looked at it intuitively, I saw that 5 years had gone by since the divorce. There were a few surgeries to correct challenges in her communication energy area, as well as wisdom energy area, along with relocation of the family.

When she finished wiping her tears, we sat in silence for what seemed to be an entire afternoon. It was important for me to hear every part of her story. All of it. She replayed every step of *the story* that was important for her. All the pieces about her feelings. In conclusion, life as she knew it had ended.

She defined the current challenges that had been looming for years to be:

- The infidelity against her created a sense of doubt within her female self

- The verbal and mental abuse she endured in the relationship collapsed her inner self, core self.

- The withholding of love and affection from her husband was confusing.

- The loss of self-identity after seemingly knowing herself.

- The loss of her financial stability after years of building and creating abundance.

- The loss of herself in the world she once knew.

- The loss of her connection to knowing how to balance herself within.

The energy of what Jenny felt was incredibly deep and very, very real. Seven years later, this story energy was still alive. It created a rise in her blood pressure as she re-lived the story. Her body trembled just as if it had happened earlier that morning or late last week. She had no idea how to move forward. She had no idea what part to fix first. Jenny had tried many different programs over the years that promised *quick* success. She had not found the answers or comfort she needed. She had not found the peace of mind that was necessary to move on.

Let's go back to the Energy Resource Chart. Imagine if Jenny wakes up in the morning with all her past disappointment, fear, and despair, what portion of her daily available energy does she have available to tackle the tasks and responsibilities of the day?

Jenny's work ahead included taking back the pieces she felt had been lost forever. Simple steps to reclaiming her self-esteem, self-assurance, self-love, and grounding herself to what she had known for over 20 years of personal accomplishment. She needed to create a balance of the years compiled together. Knowing that although these challenges she felt in her life did occur, but that the same pain and suffering she continued to endure was the exact poison that was keeping her from enjoying the remainder of her years, she needed to make a decision. Choose to move slowly back into life, replacing all the old words and thoughts with thoughts and words of her future. Or, stay there. Right there, in that place of limbo. Knowing that happiness was not available, nor was a future. Although it was difficult, living the second way would be even more difficult as she aged and her children left home. She needed to muster every ounce of courage available to start the process of moving forward. The long road to self-connection was not easy for Jenny. She continues to work on this balance even today.

We cannot forget what has happened in our life. To try is senseless. It can lead to many types of addiction challenges. We must find a way, tools, various means, whatever works for us individually to recreate and reconnect to our core self. Depending on what the story energy is, you must know that it is possible. If you are still alive, still breathing, and still have the energy in you to want a more comfortable life, filled with happiness and pleasure, then it is *absolutely possible!* Believe it!

Will we ever be *the same*? If we answer that question intellectually, then the answer is 'no.' We will never be the same. The body, mind, and spirit had an experience. Experiences, either pleasurable or unpleasant, have an effect. It is how we handle the effect that the experience had on us--that is of the most importance in healing.

Do we ever want to be the same? Maybe yes, and maybe no. We are here to experience life! We are here to feel, express, explore, take risks, and seek out what creates a sense of happiness, self-worth, comfort, and success within our own being. We cannot possibly experience life without taking risks, can we? Finding comfort and stability, after the challenges had created the most pain and discomfort, is what we can strive for. What we can fill in as we grow and learn.

As adults, and as hard as it is for us to believe, we have been given signals, signs, and feelings of *danger* from our inner self. How many of us have kept moving forward in a business situation, personal situation, relationship situation, or a situation with our families, knowing that it did not feel right for some reason? That is the feeling I want you to begin to know. To begin to embrace within yourself. Our body, our mind, and our spirit are here to assist us in creating balance in our life. Yes, to assist us in making decisions that steer us in the direction of harmony. Even though we will experience discomfort, disappointment, and pain in our lifetime, we will also experience great joy, tremendous happiness, and many different types of pleasurable moments. This is the upside of engaging in life. We cannot control what happens in life, even though we would love to. What we can do is to listen to our inner voice, our inner self. It can, and will, help us discern healthy choices and unhealthy choices. This, you can depend on.

Allow Passion to Create Your Stories!

REFRAMING STORY ENERGY

How many of you have challenges that flood your mind first thing in the morning and late at night before retiring to bed? How many have insomnia or cannot sleep comfortably through the night? When we repeat the normal patterns of life in our mind and our emotions, we start to create and live in stagnation. Stagnation of life itself and the possibilities of the future are all attached to the theme we hear and continue to hear from our thoughts and feelings of the past. If we truly want to make changes, substantial changes, with rather quick results, it is mandatory that we start to change the thoughts from the moment we have our feet hit the ground, or on the bed before we start our day.

Shifting this energy and replacing the repeated patterns of thought and communication to ourself or those who are in our life are imperative for a change to take place. It requires a commitment to live with faith and trust. You need to learn to trust yourself that. When you let go of this uncomfortable energy of thought and feeling and replace it with a healthy way of thinking and feeling, the new sensation is viable and real. When we have set up the strange habitual comfort of misery, despair, and disappointment, we must replace that pattern with one that gives us a new sense of possibilities.

Below are the steps to help you shift the story energy:

- Acknowledge each morning upon waking that you are going to shift the energy associated with the burdensome thoughts of the day.

- Breathe in deeply when you feel and hear the negative or overwhelming thought come in. Breathe in deeply, exhale, and say to yourself: "This thought does not serve me today."

- Throughout the day, when thoughts come in that are creating a sense of anxiety, anger, despair, or upset, breathe deep and do not allow it to occupy more than 5 minutes of your time. Allow the thought to release itself by acknowledging that it is no longer necessary to hold onto this feeling.

Equally important is to acknowledge. For seven days, please engage in the following acknowledgment:

- See the beauty in three different moments you encounter through visual stimulation, communication energy, or thought energy.

- Create 3 individual conversations with individuals who you are currently interacting with in your life. Express energy that produces happiness, joy, and satisfaction.

- Consciously catch yourself three times in one day, when your emotional reaction to a moment creates an imbalance within yourself. At the moment you catch yourself, acknowledge your inner power of conscious thought.

Please have faith in yourself and your ability to make these shifts. Start slow with focus. Each day find out what you can remove to unburden your energy resource. As time goes by, you will eliminate the unnecessary energy of worry, anger, despair, or uncertainty. You will fill that space of energy with hope, happiness, passion, and a sense of self-confidence.

If your personal story energy involves the following, please start to work on balancing the individual energy center associated with the imbalance:

Finances: Look at passion energy, self-assurance energy, or stability energy. Find out the *root* cause of the challenge.

Emotional challenges: Look at love energy, self-confidence energy, or communication energy. This challenge is also linked to the passion energy.

Career or work-related challenges: Look at communication energy, self-assurance energy, or passion energy.

Childhood challenges: Look at stability energy, heart energy, wisdom energy, or self-assurance energy.

Health and wellness challenges: Look at stability energy, intuitive energy, communication energy, and passion energy.

Affirmations are very important for movement. You must repeat through thoughts, words, and expression what you want to feel and have in your life. If you feel you are stuck in a particular area, write down a few affirmations that you feel connected to. You must believe the affirmation for the energy to attach itself to you. Ask yourself what energy is needed to support change in an area of challenge. When you ask the question, write down the answer you hear and feel from your intuitive energy. When this practice becomes an automatic routine, as automatic as brushing your teeth and brushing your hair, you will start to *feel* the empowerment connection to your own energy self. It is powerful!

The First Thought of the Day

How can this happen? It must happen with the first thoughts of the day. It must begin with acknowledgment when the thought first comes into the mind. Replacing this first thought with a more attractive thought will immediately give you the chance to move forward. For example, say that you are concerned about your finances. Bills are piled up and the pressure is all too consuming. When the thought comes into your energy self about the bills, the fear, the financial pressure, the idea that you cannot make it another day, you breathe and begin the shift. You must immediately change the story.

Even if it is as simple as: "Today is a day I can rest from my financial worry. Support is on its way." Please at least give it a try. I know this is very difficult for many people to think this can possibly help, but it can. Trust that the words, phrases, and thoughts you have each day hold an enormous amount of energy. Practice this often and you will experience just what I describe herein.

The first step is to believe; have faith that even though you are not completely sure of *how* you will create financial stability, *you will*. *When we start to create the reasons, it will not happen*; you have just created the energy that will promote it not to happen. Energy is energy. Plan to accept and create as much as you can imagine and dream from your thoughts. I cannot reiterate this enough to you. You must acknowledge how powerful your thoughts are.

Remind yourself of the *energy resource* we each have available to us. Each morning, you must maximize the energy you have available to you. Increase the energy resources for your day by acknowledging what you do not have time to think about. Determine what you can live without. Find the obstacles in your mind that create a sense of fatigue, a feeling of being overwhelmed, and the cause of stagnation. Mental stagnation creates loss of energy.

As you start this process, which may take practice, you will find your energy, inter-action with daily life, and the start of building a new future of possibilities just *an energetic shift away!* Don't give up!

Your New Life Awaits You!

EPILOGUE

Sitting in my chair observing, feeling, and seeing from my position, I have for many years wanted to help! Prior to embarking on this unique journey as an intuitive, I was in the personnel business, helping those who needed employment, career change, and the confidence to move into the next phase of their lives. In some capacity, from my youth as an English teacher working with foreign students or refugees, I have been teaching.

After years of discovery, I have found a way to reach and teach a larger audience than within my private practice or as a participant in the clinic where I currently work. I set out on the path to publish my ideas, thoughts, and experiences. For the past 5 years, I have been actively pursuing more connection to the real essence of the 7 major energy centers. I have been taking notes, gathering patterns, and asking very direct questions. I wanted to bring the energy centers to the forefront of my focus to help those looking for deeper answers to life challenges. Many people have ideas and conclusions about the chakras. I believe that my unique ability as an accomplished intuitive has allowed me to finally express my unique interpretation and application of my recent insights and findings within these pages. With the help of those very special individuals I have worked with over the years, the accumulation of all I have learned, we together may shed some light on *'the energy of life'* we are all involved with as human beings.

Although the *chakra* concept has been around for over 2000 years and it has gained some ground, it is not easily accessed unless you have engaged in the Yoga Community at some point in your life. I have created a simple concept using words and charts that is easily identifiable to those without a yoga background. My attempt at making it as simple and readable as possible may have a huge influence on those who seek a deeper understanding of challenges that they can easily and clearly identify within themselves.

If it is your intention, your true intention, to understand more about your own wisdom, your own connection to the energy in your life, *The Energy of Life* will wake you up to the moment, to today, and to your life. You will take from it as much as you need to understand more about yourself. But it is not a *fix all.*

Life is not to be fixed, nor to be avoided.

Life is an experience.

It is a wonderful experience filled with many opportunities, feelings, choices, and outcomes. How we interact in life, how we see the moments, how we embrace those who come to us, how we love and accept those in our life, how we see ourselves, I believe these are all areas of our responsibilities. And by that I mean to *respond* with *ability*. Life has many sides to explore. Remember, life is constantly moving. How we interact and react to our life is in direct alignment with the joy, passion, happiness, and contentment we will feel.

The biggest challenge people have in learning something new is the need to know it all and know it now. I am always asked, "How fast will this work?" I recommend that you take healing, empowerment, and movement, *as slow as you can*. Speed it up when you feel that you are able and take the time necessary to heal or mend, even when it is taking longer than you would like. I want to remind you that life is not a race. It is an experience filled with moments. Moments that need to be savored. When you are sick or feel down, why do you want to rush yourself back to health? Why not just take a moment and *feel* why the body is responding with illness? Why not try to get to know what is really going on around you in your life? Try to *live* in life, acknowledge life, and participate in life fully! The energy of life is electrifying....believe this! Move through it as gently and compassionately as you are able.

We can often wonder why we are not healing. We wonder why all that we are doing and practicing and swallowing are not working fast enough. We worry. Why do other people seem to get better faster than us, and why do we stay *sick* for months or years? Please remember that each of us, as individuals, is all learning at our own pace. We are processing as fast as we are able. We have unique conditions in our psyche that our friends, neighbors, and colleagues do not share. We even have personal life challenges that those in our household experience quite differently.

Life Is an Individual Experience for All of Us

Find your inner resources. Find your inner path. Find your truth. This is your life. Find what works for you with what you have experienced in your lifetime. *Do not compare* your healing or empowerment with those around you. Take the time you need to process what you are learning and feeling. Do not set your goals, standards, or dreams based upon anyone else's ideas or expectation! Find your own voice, your own inner knowing!

Timing is of the essence. If you believe that we are here learning, growing, and perhaps having a life purpose, then you will also understand that we each interact in our life while we learn lessons, experience moments, and until the process is finished, we stay right where we need to be. We do not need to be rushed. We do not need to be like others. We do not need to follow the path that is not ours to travel. Remind yourself of that often.

You can, and will, help yourself if it is truly your intention. This book of information and tools can provide you with the security, self-confidence, and inner trust that will lead you to your own self-discovery. The connection to the very powerful you!

Our body, our mind, and our senses have everything stored in a place which can be accessed and implemented when you know how. Our body responds to our truth. There is a spiritual component, a consciousness, for each individual human being, one that is waiting to serve. The energy centers in the body have information and power to help you find your way.

May I Leave You With This…

I believe that deep inside ourself, we know the truth about ourself, our wants and needs and what we are here to accomplish. Please know we as a human race, as individuals, have not entered a race. We are not being judged by anyone but ourself. We know our background, our family, our likes and our dislikes. We know what creates happiness within us, and we know what creates a great deal of stress and strife. Do not allow anyone to take away your wisdom, insight, and knowing.....it came with you and will surely leave with you.

This is your life. Move through it at your pace. Slow down. Look around. Even though in the past you have believed that you could not make a change, dig deep inside to find the courage, the confidence, to seek out what you truly want to create and delete in your life. Do not be afraid. Find your comfort zone. Find your truth so that you are able to communicate and share it with others. I know you are something quite spectacular! Each person I have had the opportunity to work with or engage with in my lifetime is special. Each has such a unique style and energy. Look inside yourself. Find the power and wisdom of yourself. I promise you, whoever you are, it is there. We are here for a very brief period of time. Please enjoy being you! It will be over before you know it.....that is a guarantee!

PERSONAL STORIES FROM COURAGEOUS INDIVIDUALS HITTING LIFE HEAD ON!

Books can be tricky. From the author's point of view, it is the truth from their perspective. Everything that is written is certainly subjective from many angles. To provide greater insight from those sitting across the desk from me, I have asked a few people I have worked with over the years if they would like to share their personal story with the audience of this book. The question was very simple: What did you learn from the experience with Jennifer? The following courageous souls filled in the blanks. We have included their photos. We collectively agreed that "seeing" the person telling their story would give greater empowerment to the experience and the feelings associated with it.

I hope you will enjoy their stories. The powerful shift they have made on the road to self-empowerment is truthful, and hopefully will inspire you.

Meet Susan

Entering my thirties was not all that it was cracked up to be. I was a professional athlete who kept having injury after injury. I went through a divorce right before my 30th birthday and my dog died of cancer at the same time. I also went through a big move from Lake Tahoe to Santa Barbara knowing not one person. And, I was diagnosed with chronic fatigue and early signs of menopause.

I was a lost soul roaming around and I happened to be talking to a friend who introduced me to Jennifer. That was the day my life started to turn around. Jennifer taught me how to slow down as she said, "Take time to smell the roses and take time to appreciate who you are. Yes, the beautiful, strong, and independent woman that you are!" She worked with me through hormone problems, my career, and life changes. In the process, I learned how to work through each energy center and focused on healing from within. I worked on taking away all the negative energy and filling and surrounding myself with positive energy! I really learned how to re-prioritize my life and become closer with God.

Before I had met Jennifer, I was running away from things in my past and, through sports, became reckless and started getting hurt. I would never stop to let my body heal. I didn't really care about my body and the harm that I was causing myself. My injuries were compounding and the numbers of surgeries were such that it was becoming ridiculous. My body had started to shut down and my hormones were all out of whack. I was told that I would never become pregnant because I had gone into early stages of menopause at 31!

When I finally started to listen to Jennifer, and started to believe in myself again, and follow the work she told me to do, a funny thing started to happen. I started to feel better and have more energy, and in turn, became happier.

I had another completely different career change and came full circle to where I began when I was little--riding horses. Horses were always my biggest passion and now I am back riding hunter jumpers as my full time job.

Then, the best gift I could have ever asked for happened…..
I am now a proud mother to a beautiful and healthy 9 months old boy! Now, this is truly living!!!!!!!

Susan

Professional Athlete and Mommy

California, USA

Meet Kimberley

The first time I spoke with Jennifer was nothing less than incredible. I contacted her because I was at a very low point in my life. I had years of negative energy built up from not speaking my truth, lack of confidence, and poor health. At the time, I was experiencing challenges that were preventing me from fully living my life, including a constant fear of dying from my health issues. Jennifer completely blew my socks off. She was not given any information about me and/or my husband other than my name and a photo, yet she knew me like a book. She even knew things about my husband and kids and was 100% accurate!

First, she calmed me down and explained that none of my health challenges were life threatening and that I was really very healthy. Just as the physicians had told me over the years. She was able to point out to me specific dates and times in my life when events happened that triggered the negative energy, negative emotions, and health problems I was experiencing. She knew things about me that no one else knew and I was so grateful when she showed me what challenges I had in my life that caused me to fill with negative energy, ultimately wiping out my nervous system.

Jennifer gave me some simple tools to use to help balance my health challenges. She also gave me great advice on how to change my energy from negative to positive. Together, we built a plan so that I could take back my life again and move forward. Most of all, she helped me truly understand why my life had been such an awful mess and how I needed to be mindful of my participation in the outcome and build up that had resulted in a huge imbalance for me and my family.

Before I spoke with Jennifer, I was stuck in a very bad place. Not only was I unable to move forward but also I had not enjoyed my life in over 10 years. Jennifer helped build hope and excitement for a future and got me moving again.

The biggest lesson she taught me is that "healing is 80% emotional and only 20% medicine and/or doctors." I am happy to admit that I am fully responsible for creating the life that I wish to have.

Kimberly Palm
Marketing Representative
West Coast

Meet Robin

I was born into an imperfect world with an imbalanced heart. The trials and tribulations on my path led me into a life of pure synchronicity filled with beautiful experiences and many wonderful teachers.

No one has been able to see me as clearly as Jennifer Kaye. With open heart surgery at the age of 4 and many doctors questioning my health from this young age, I was conditioned to believe that I was powerless to heal myself.

For most of my life, I was in search of a way to listen to my inner guidance and remind myself that I have everything I need. Conscious breathing has been the most powerful tool that I have found to integrate the trauma and stress of life and eliminate those physical symptoms that were created.

Jennifer is the only person I have trusted as much as my own breath for guidance and support; we instantly connected from our first exchange and I was amazed by her ability to feel so very clearly and know the deepest root cause of the imbalances held in the energy body. She confirmed the power of the breath as one of the most effective tools she had ever experienced and began to offer me clear guidance on how to create more harmony, love, and abundance in my life.

Over the years, Jennifer has helped me cultivate a nurturing and loving relationship with myself by giving me a very comfortable direction in times of challenge and confusion. She has been an angel of guiding clarity and confirmation in my life. Her ability to see things as they really are and to feel what is in or out of alignment with our highest good and greatest well being is a knack that some people only claim to have. Jennifer shares this wisdom with passion and humility. She has helped me use a once wounded heart to root deeply into my true nature as a loving servant devoted to the reminder of the breath.

It is a great honor that fulfills my purpose today to teach 'The Energy of Life,' to be able to meet people where they are at and help empower them to decide what healing options are best for them.

Jennifer lives from the heart. In a world of illusion and confusion, it is rare to find such a gifted healer and teacher who is not here for herself, but rather has accepted a role to help others with a genuine sense of caring, understanding, and love.

Robin Clements

Founder, Baja Wellness, Baja Mexico

Breath Coach Facilitator/International Speaker-Educator

Master Teacher/Trainer of 'The Energy of Life'

Meet Matti

First, let me say that I am so grateful to have met Jennifer when I did and to have her be a part of my life. Through my work with Jennifer, I learned about my energy and how it affects everything in my life.

I learned about positive and negative energy and how to recognize it. I learned how my past experiences and the way in which I dealt (or didn't deal) with them affected my later life.

Jennifer and I proceeded to do a lot of energy center work and, through her Energy Center Program, I then began to understand the energy related to each center and how to tap into each center on my own as I needed, and, more importantly, to understand that the balance of all the energy centers was vital for healthy living.

Jennifer helped me understand that the choices I make are guided by my intuition and that I could continue to trust my intuition. She guided me through a very difficult period of my life by helping me understand that it was okay to trust my feelings.

I learned to slow down and to trust my inner self. I learned to always be honest with everyone and never to compromise myself or my needs. I learned that all energy in this universe inter-connects and to be aware of it at all times.

Take nothing for granted.

Today, my life is so different, so wonderful and balanced. I continued to re-visit my material from Jennifer and reflect on all of our sessions. She truly is an amazing gifted and sincere individual who has an uncanny way of reaching each person she works with.

Matti Bourgault

International VP / Consultant Retail Industry

North America, Pacific Rim

Meet Donna

I respectfully met Jennifer in 2006. I was given her name by a massage therapist. I held on to that name for awhile, but finally decided to call her and she just happened to pick up the phone. She said to drop on by and so I did, and that is how a new journey began for me.

It was imperative that I find a way to separate the environment I worked in with the personal life I wanted to have. My job is very demanding and not always a positive work environment. Very high stress levels are brought on by the interaction with others. I needed to find a way to become more balanced within my own psyche. The environment was affecting my health and my emotional stability.

Jennifer immediately brought to my attention the negative energy that surrounded me, mostly due to my job and the way I dealt with energy in general. She assisted me to be more aware of the different areas from my past and how they affect the present. As she increased my awareness of the energy centers and what they represented, I was able to deal with my own thoughts and actions.

I obtained a better understanding that a person creates their own reality and that I could balance myself through the awareness of my energy centers. As we worked through each center I was brought to an understanding of clarity and clearing. By bringing attention to myself and the energies that I had been holding onto for so long, it helped me grow tremendously.

Affirmations and oils helped me on a daily basis; they helped open portals to my true potential. I now use this knowledge daily, trusting my intuition and knowing when I need to ground and listen to my highest self.

Donna O

Law Enforcement

West Coast, USA

Meet Tom

My experience with Jennifer is as follows:

Firstly, I encountered life.

When I began working with Jennifer, I had no idea I would be diagnosed with cancer, that I would undergo radical surgery (and still have cancer), that deeply loved family and extended family members would also either be diagnosed with cancer or soon fall dead, unceremoniously and alone. I had no idea that my partner would be traumatized by severe false allegations that would tear his family apart. He and I had no idea that our lives would be forever changed by this complex and elegantly swift thing called....life. With all in the space of one year.

To say that I encountered huge overwhelm while working with Jennifer would be a cosmic understatement.

However, to say that I encountered a clear, focused, unflinching, loving, tough coach, clairvoyant, and colleague, would be spot on!

Did I mention my fears? My strengths? My doubts? My cynicism? My hostilities? My creativity? My resilience and my capacity for growth and love? Not only did I encounter all of these, but I also re-discovered the broader spectrum of "me-at-this-moment."

It was as if Jennifer accessed a bottle of psychic window cleaner, sprayed it into the great panes of my soul, and began wiping away the decades of grime that prevented others from seeing in and me seeing out.

I believe that I have greater clarity now: a few tools for maintaining my inner upkeep and a better sense of the vast possibilities of my life.

Re-learning that human energy is a limited and precious commodity not only resonated with my training as an analytically-informed psychotherapist (reference Freud), but it also helped me build a more mature respect and humility for the mind, body, and emotions.

And finally, I learned that trust goes a long way!

Tom Price

Licensed Psychotherapist - Case Manager

State of Washington

Meet Yimin's Son

Several months ago I needed help with my son who was suffering from severe allergies. He was only 5 months old. He had been admitted to the local emergency room many times and was very sick.

I heard about Jennifer because she is in the clinic where my dad works. I called on her.

My son had not slept a full night since he was born. His body had such severe eczema and heat that he had holes erupting from his skin. His body was always hot and flushed and he could not pass bowel movements.

Jennifer was able to provide information about the heat in my son's body, the congestion with his intake of liquid, and a formula that was harmful, even though she had never met my son. He was not present during the consultation. Within the first

24 hours following her suggestion, my son was no longer in discomfort.

I learned about the sensitivity of my son's stomach and his inability to process many types of food. I also learned that my son was very nervous around loud noise and disruption. The anxiousness he felt disrupted his sleep and his nervous system directly affected his stomach, colon, and intestines.

I'm aware today that I must listen to my son's cry when he is being fed--that his nervous system and digestive track is linked very closely. I'm very grateful for Jennifer's willingness to share her powerful gift with those who are in desperate need of answers.

Yimin

Real Estate Broker

Pacific Rim & Washington State

Meet Stephen

When I met Jennifer, I was not seeking direction or help. I believed that it was by chance. But I know now that it was not by chance that I was able to sit down with Jennifer.

During my first unofficial meeting with Jennifer, she began to explain several things regarding how I had felt inside but did not know why or how to apply the sensations and thoughts I had running through my mind. After listening to Jennifer's opinion regarding various sensations that I have experienced over the past few years, many things just started to click.

From a young age, I knew that I was quite different from those who surrounded me. I had the ability to sort things out differently than others. And even though I did not fully understand the implications of what I felt and knew, I knew it was a natural sense. I recently learned it is a strong sense of empathy with a keen sense of insight. Something I have used during several years of my teaching and coaching to guide me with my students.

Through my time with Jennifer, I can confidently say I know now that the energy in my life, my perception of the energy, and my reaction to the energy all have affected me. I have learned through processing the information given to me by Jennifer that I have a choice in what I get involved in. I have a choice with every opportunity and experience that comes my way. Listening to my inner voice is now quite helpful. It is a tool that has become automatic for me.

Truth be known, I had no idea what energy was or really meant, nor the effect it has on us. Although it made perfect sense, her words of wisdom or intellect is not information or theories you hear every day. But from watching my interactions with others or sitting for a moment when I feel a sensation, it now makes perfect sense. I am clearly aware of much more than I have ever been aware of.

I have learned that when I experience feelings in my stomach which I've had since an early age, it is my own self allowing me to know the truth about how I am feeling. My stomach is a focal point for me now. I understand that I can rely on the feelings that I have. In Jennifer's words, "…..self-assurance energy."

I'm looking forward to taking this information into my future, benefiting both my personal and professional relationships.

Stephen Potter

International Sports Coach/Trainer/Teacher

Leeds Metropolitan University, Leeds, England

ACKNOWLEDGMENTS

My Mother: I want to thank my mother for her incredible *love and support*. Without her capacity to love me unconditionally, I would have missed out on many opportunities that took me to places of grace and beauty. Judy Kay Robinson is an incredible human being.

Because of her natural gift as a clairvoyant, with professional accomplishments in an industry that is often quite misunderstood, I had the opportunity, after gaining personal confidence, to develop and apply my own gift. I thank her for giving me the life that allows me to showcase my special talent. I love you, mom.

My Daughter: At a very young age, I knew that I would be having a very special person come into my life, my daughter. The day she was born, I looked into her face and sang the "Joe Crocker" song, "You Are So Beautiful." I continue singing that song to her today! My daughter is a treasure. She has supported me unconditionally throughout our entire relationship. I love you, Maggie!

My Family: My family holds *so many* memories for me. *Six* children in all, we are different in so many ways. What we are able to teach one another, sometimes feels free and easy and sometimes painful, but always purposeful. We are able to *show up*, show affection, voice our opinions, and, at the end of it all, remain intact. It hasn't been simple or easy as we all know in interacting with families.

My dad, Dwain, passed away a few years ago and I want to acknowledge his presence in my life. The love, affection, and all that I learned from him remains a staple in my life. My brother Wes holds a very special place in my heart. We've had so many challenges growing into ourselves and yet, at the bottom, I feel we are the most alike. My sister Kellie has had the toughest of roads in this lifetime. She is my special teacher. My beautiful and talented nephews and nieces (with 4 great nieces and a great nephew), including Billy who is no longer with us; they continue to add happiness, hope, and joy to my life. I feel so grateful for my family and have always felt that no matter what our different paths, our beliefs, and our personal struggles are, we're never further than a phone call away.

Meaningful Relationships: How can I thank all the people who have supported my spirit without dedicating an entire chapter to the entire experience of my relationships. I've been blessed with an incredible collection of friendships that seem so *auspicious*. People come in and out of our lives teaching us during moments of unexpected support. Sometimes we want them to stay forever and they simply can't. They arrive right on the *cue* and sometimes leave as quickly as they arrive. The creator, god. Thank you for encouraging and supporting my life energy. Big 'B' my very best friend, Byron Moreno, has been a pillar of stability throughout my entire life. Jerry Moreno, always there. Sharon Kerr, always keeping things moving. Joe Pagano for teaching me about friendship. Donna for her presence. Robert Rothbard, true companionship, extending family energy during a very difficult time. Kimberly Jackson, maintaining the "wild boar/Virgo" energy. Phyllis Noble for sharing my gift with her intimate community. Gen Takahashi for providing love and support at a very sensitive time. Cannot forget Mer, Matti, and the many others who have touched my life in so many meaningful ways.

I want to personally thank from the bottom of my heart, Ms. Ilene Segalove. Her perseverance in keeping me in line, on task, and moving forward while writing this book has been quite the inspiration. She is one amazingly talented woman!

The people who have called on me for the past 13 years to provide assistance using my unique gift, thank you! I want to personally thank all of you for believing in me and encouraging my growth! I hope you continue to grow using all you have learned about the personal power inside and your individual gifts.

And finally, my son, Matthew, for bringing his incredible energy to our family. What a huge surprise...his arrival! Without him and his incredible spirit, life as I know it today would have a huge gap! His light shines so bright and so brilliantly. I love you, Matt!!

I've learned throughout the incredible journey of my very unique and special life that when we allow the lessons, the feelings, the opportunities to be just that, they certainly will. But, when we don't want the opportunities to show up, they don't wait for us to give permission; if the movement needs to take place, it will arrive with or without notice! Acceptance and compassion.

I appreciate those who have stayed for many, many years and those who come around to teach me and then get on with their own process and life. That being said, I want to *thank* everyone who has shown up to teach, support, and take me to the next phase of my life. It's been quite a ride for both you and me!!

ABOUT THE AUTHOR

Jennifer Kaye was born into a family with a deeply intuitive mother. Her home life was anything but normal, and she grew up in an environment that was not easily understood nor accepted by the outside world. In Southern California, Jennifer's mother worked along side law enforcement officials using her clairvoyant talents to work on and solve numerous serious criminal cases. Jennifer respected her mother's important contributions, but found growing up in this out of the ordinary world terribly stressful. From an early age, she shut the door to the world of intangible phenomena and chose to inhabit the realm of the intellect. As a young adult, she immersed herself in the corporate world where she was extremely successful, still avoiding accessing her own clairvoyant gifts passed down to her from three generations.

Eventually, Jennifer had a change of heart and mind. She began to recognize her profound ability to see into the physical body and was inspired to dive into a deep study of science and medicine to augment her intuitive skills. She also began to embrace and acknowledge her calling to help those who needed healing on all levels of being. Still, she hesitated before stepping into the controversial realm of working with her extraordinary abilities. At the end of many sessions in her first year working as an intuitive, she'd laugh and say, "Yes, I used to have a real job." In spite of the push-pull, Jennifer found her work was life changing both for herself and others and knew she had to follow her path.

That was 13 years ago and a lot has changed! Jennifer Kaye is now a well-known and respected leader in the field of clairvoyant intuition. She has built a solid and elegant platform of information and experience with tools and techniques that educate her clients so that they can gain self-confidence, hope, clarity, and ultimately healing from the inside out.

Her work is greeted with respect by prestigious medical clinics, scientific environments, funded research projects, licensed health care professionals, and most recently within the mental health community.

Jennifer Kaye splits her time between the Pacific Northwest and British Columbia with her two children. She has a private practice in Bellevue, Washington and travels the globe teaching her Empowerment Programs.

THE TEAM:

Robin Clements

Robin learned to "feel" his way through traditional Western medicine and Eastern rooted natural and non-invasive medicine since his early ages due to the health issue he was born with, underwent open heart surgery at the age of 4. This has led him to connect to his "god" given talent of being of service to others and understand himself and his role as a natural born leader/teacher.

Robin holds a doctorate of Divinity which allows him to perform spiritual ceremonies that includes marital services. He is a Sr. Trainer and Facilitator of The Transformational Breath

Foundation, and has been certified to teach breath work Internationally by Dr. Judith Kravitz. He is certified as a Yoga Instructor by Exhale Center for Sacred Movement, a Yoga Alliance Registered School, and is an assistant to his teacher Shiva Rea. Each of these positions holds a sacred place in Robin's life.

When Robin met Jennifer Kaye in 2004, there was an instant and deep connection between both of them. Over the years, Jennifer devoted time and energy to expand Robin's conscious and unconscious understanding of energy and how it affects the mind, body, and spirit. In 2010, Robin became Jennifer's first Teacher/Trainer of the "Energy of Life" work. Today Robin is a Senior Master Trainer and travels throughout Asia, Europe, Latin America and Canada, teaching the "Energy of Life" workshops.

Robin is also the Founder and Director of Baja Wellness in Los Cabos, B.C.S., Mexico. When in town, Robin offers weekly classes of the Breath Wave Experience, Vinyasa Wave Flow Yoga and shares one Trance Dance ritual every month. He maintains the main healing space at Raices y Brazos as he is also certified in the arts of Watsu, Alphabiotics, Postural Integration, La Stone Therapy, Thai Massage, and Visionary Cranial Sacral Therapy.

Robin's breath related CD's are available at www.jenniferkaye.com under Robin. His work includes: 'Introduction to Transformational Breathing', '108 Breaths for Daily Living,' and a full guided "Transformational Breath Wave Experience."

Dr. Huy Hoang, MD

After Dr. Hoang received his bachelor degree from MIT in Electrical Engineering, he went on to obtain his medical degree from University of Maryland. His research in the area of free radicals and drug metabolism and toxicity were received with honors from NIH and University of Maryland, respectively. He gained his medical specialist from UCLA, which including acupuncture, and Olive View Medical Center. Later, he has become interested in the alternative medicine and nutrition areas. Realizing that the mind, body and spirit are tightly connected, he left the Medical Group of Beverly Hills to open his own Natural Health Medical Center. For the past twenty years, Dr. Hoang has dedicated his life to providing the best possible medical treatment he is capable of extending. Dr. Hoang's education, insight, and desire to be of service to others earn him his natural ability to find the core issue surrounding his patients' immediate health challenge.

Dr. Hoang's private practice is located in Los Angeles, California.

Please feel free to contact Dr. Hoang in person or by phone:

Natural Health Medical Center, Inc.

4469 Redondo Beach Blvd, Lawndale, CA. 90260

Tel: 310-479-2266

drhoang@naturalhealthmc.com

Thitiwan Buranachokpaisan, Ph.D.

Thitiwan Buranachokpaisan received her pharmacy degree from Chiangmai University in Thailand. She later received her master's and doctorate degree in Pharmaceutical Sciences from Rutgers University, NJ, with her thesis research focused in the area of microemulsion formulation and hepatotoxicity of reactive metabolites, respectively. She has broad experiences in working on various types of cosmetic formulations, including handling of all technical challenges of the products through the launching stage. Thitiwan bears a strong expertise in the injectable pharmaceutical dosage formulas, with extensive experiences in lyophilization technology, scale-up, and development activities from early phase to clinical studies. Thitiwan holds several formulation patents through her years of working in the cosmetic and pharmaceutical fields. Her life-long core interest is working on developing innovative and sustainable protocol for our health and well being, through identifying and utilizing complementary aspects of concepts in different disciplines.

Please feel free to contact Dr. Thitiwan at www.jenniferkaye.com

JENNIFER KAYE EMPOWERMENT COLLECTION:

The Jennifer Kaye Line promotes personal empowerment utilizing natural resources. You can find the following at her website:

- Empowerment Jewelry-Semi Precious Stones; 7 Energy Center Necklaces and Bracelets
- Organic T-Shirts, Hoodies, and Bags
- Organic Energy Center Essences - Organic Essence Blends for balancing, recharging, and alignment
- Empowerment Sachets and Pillows - Organic Lavender and Rose
- Notebooks, Journals, and Calendars - supporting self-empowerment
- CD - Affirmation Techniques by Jennifer Kaye
- CD - Instructional: Balancing the Energy Centers with Jennifer Kaye
- Book: The Energy of Life - A guide to Healing and Balancing from Within

JENNIFER KAYE
Mind Body Spirit Connection

www.jenniferkaye.com

Vibrational Necklaces & Bracelets

Organic Lavender Sachets

Organic Essences Natures Scents

222   The Energy of Life

JENNIFER KAYE

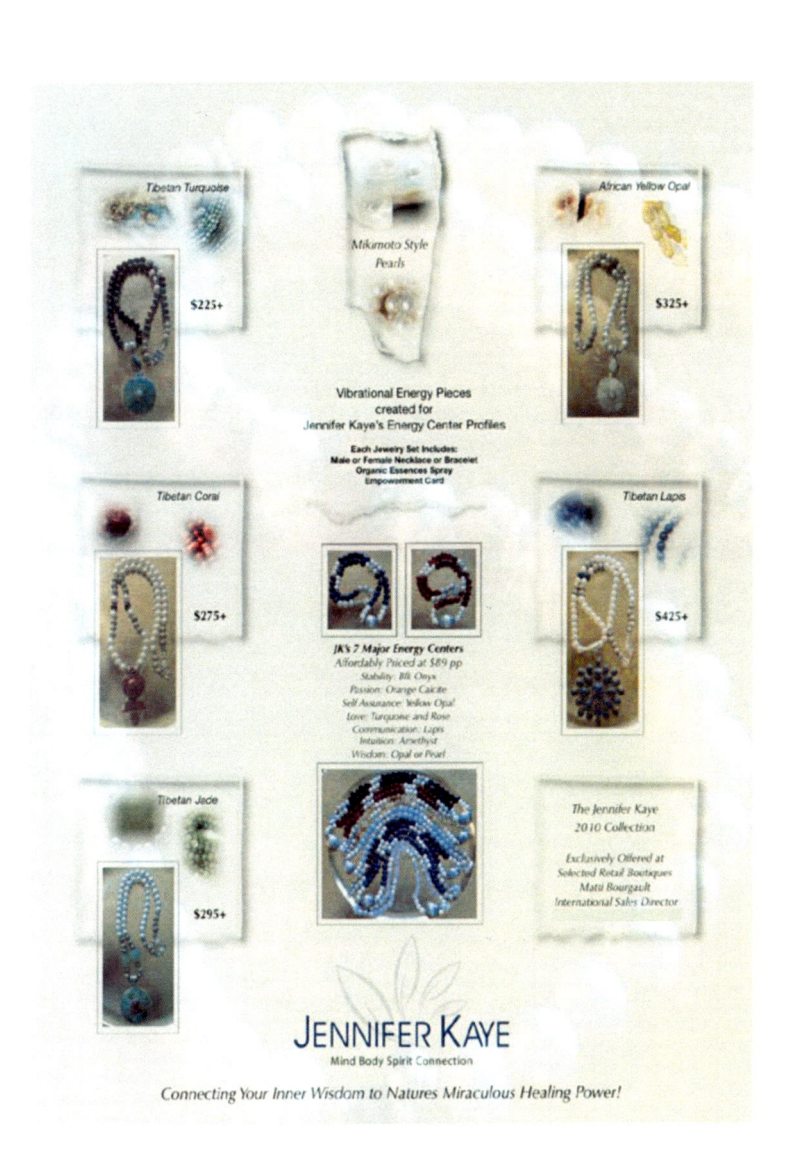